THIS IS YOUR **PASSBOOK**® FOR ...

PROPERTY CLERK

NLC®

NATIONAL LEARNING CORPORATION®

passbooks.com

PASSBOOK® SERIES

THE *PASSBOOK® SERIES* has been created to prepare applicants and candidates for the ultimate academic battlefield – the examination room.

At some time in our lives, each and every one of us may be required to take an examination – for validation, matriculation, admission, qualification, registration, certification, or licensure.

Based on the assumption that every applicant or candidate has met the basic formal educational standards, has taken the required number of courses, and read the necessary texts, the *PASSBOOK® SERIES* furnishes the one special preparation which may assure passing with confidence, instead of failing with insecurity. Examination questions – together with answers – are furnished as the basic vehicle for study so that the mysteries of the examination and its compounding difficulties may be eliminated or diminished by a sure method.

This book is meant to help you pass your examination provided that you qualify and are serious in your objective.

The entire field is reviewed through the huge store of content information which is succinctly presented through a provocative and challenging approach – the question-and-answer method.

A climate of success is established by furnishing the correct answers at the end of each test.

You soon learn to recognize types of questions, forms of questions, and patterns of questioning. You may even begin to anticipate expected outcomes.

You perceive that many questions are repeated or adapted so that you can gain acute insights, which may enable you to score many sure points.

You learn how to confront new questions, or types of questions, and to attack them confidently and work out the correct answers.

You note objectives and emphases, and recognize pitfalls and dangers, so that you may make positive educational adjustments.

Moreover, you are kept fully informed in relation to new concepts, methods, practices, and directions in the field.

You discover that you arre actually taking the examination all the time: you are preparing for the examination by "taking" an examination, not by reading extraneous and/or supererogatory textbooks.

In short, this PASSBOOK®, used directedly, should be an important factor in helping you to pass your test.

PROPERTY CLERK

DUTIES

Receives money, valuables, and other articles seized as evidence, removed from prisoners, or lost or stolen property recovered by police; prepares typewritten record of articles and valuables received and files it in a cross index file; attaches a consecutive number tag to all articles and stores them in property bins; places all valuables, narcotics, and firearms in a safe or in specially designated areas; notifies owners by mail of property being held and releases property according to established procedures; receives custody of evidence to be used in court and is responsible for safekeeping; maintains records of property and evidence; receives fines or fees for impounded automobiles, issues receipts, and records information on cards; records bids and collects money received at auto pound auctions; moves and arranges unclaimed property, such as bicycles, in preparation for public auction and participates in property auctions; takes yearly inventory of property in storage areas and prepares reports for Property Clerk; inputs and retrieves various types of information on CRT using codes and reference materials; sweeps and maintains storage areas.

SCOPE OF THE EXAMINATION

The multiple-choice written test will cover knowledge, skills, and/or abilities in such areas as:
1. Storeskeeping and inventory control;
2. Keeping simple inventory records;
3. Name and number checking; and
4. Coding/decoding information.

HOW TO TAKE A TEST

I. YOU MUST PASS AN EXAMINATION

A. *WHAT EVERY CANDIDATE SHOULD KNOW*

Examination applicants often ask us for help in preparing for the written test. What can I study in advance? What kinds of questions will be asked? How will the test be given? How will the papers be graded?

As an applicant for a civil service examination, you may be wondering about some of these things. Our purpose here is to suggest effective methods of advance study and to describe civil service examinations.

Your chances for success on this examination can be increased if you know how to prepare. Those "pre-examination jitters" can be reduced if you know what to expect. You can even experience an adventure in good citizenship if you know why civil service exams are given.

B. *WHY ARE CIVIL SERVICE EXAMINATIONS GIVEN?*

Civil service examinations are important to you in two ways. As a citizen, you want public jobs filled by employees who know how to do their work. As a job seeker, you want a fair chance to compete for that job on an equal footing with other candidates. The best-known means of accomplishing this two-fold goal is the competitive examination.

Exams are widely publicized throughout the nation. They may be administered for jobs in federal, state, city, municipal, town or village governments or agencies.

Any citizen may apply, with some limitations, such as the age or residence of applicants. Your experience and education may be reviewed to see whether you meet the requirements for the particular examination. When these requirements exist, they are reasonable and applied consistently to all applicants. Thus, a competitive examination may cause you some uneasiness now, but it is your privilege and safeguard.

C. *HOW ARE CIVIL SERVICE EXAMS DEVELOPED?*

Examinations are carefully written by trained technicians who are specialists in the field known as "psychological measurement," in consultation with recognized authorities in the field of work that the test will cover. These experts recommend the subject matter areas or skills to be tested; only those knowledges or skills important to your success on the job are included. The most reliable books and source materials available are used as references. Together, the experts and technicians judge the difficulty level of the questions.

Test technicians know how to phrase questions so that the problem is clearly stated. Their ethics do not permit "trick" or "catch" questions. Questions may have been tried out on sample groups, or subjected to statistical analysis, to determine their usefulness.

Written tests are often used in combination with performance tests, ratings of training and experience, and oral interviews. All of these measures combine to form the best-known means of finding the right person for the right job.

II. HOW TO PASS THE WRITTEN TEST

A. NATURE OF THE EXAMINATION

To prepare intelligently for civil service examinations, you should know how they differ from school examinations you have taken. In school you were assigned certain definite pages to read or subjects to cover. The examination questions were quite detailed and usually emphasized memory. Civil service exams, on the other hand, try to discover your present ability to perform the duties of a position, plus your potentiality to learn these duties. In other words, a civil service exam attempts to predict how successful you will be. Questions cover such a broad area that they cannot be as minute and detailed as school exam questions.

In the public service similar kinds of work, or positions, are grouped together in one "class." This process is known as *position-classification*. All the positions in a class are paid according to the salary range for that class. One class title covers all of these positions, and they are all tested by the same examination.

B. FOUR BASIC STEPS

1) Study the announcement

How, then, can you know what subjects to study? Our best answer is: "Learn as much as possible about the class of positions for which you've applied." The exam will test the knowledge, skills and abilities needed to do the work.

Your most valuable source of information about the position you want is the official exam announcement. This announcement lists the training and experience qualifications. Check these standards and apply only if you come reasonably close to meeting them.

The brief description of the position in the examination announcement offers some clues to the subjects which will be tested. Think about the job itself. Review the duties in your mind. Can you perform them, or are there some in which you are rusty? Fill in the blank spots in your preparation.

Many jurisdictions preview the written test in the exam announcement by including a section called "Knowledge and Abilities Required," "Scope of the Examination," or some similar heading. Here you will find out specifically what fields will be tested.

2) Review your own background

Once you learn in general what the position is all about, and what you need to know to do the work, ask yourself which subjects you already know fairly well and which need improvement. You may wonder whether to concentrate on improving your strong areas or on building some background in your fields of weakness. When the announcement has specified "some knowledge" or "considerable knowledge," or has used adjectives like "beginning principles of..." or "advanced ... methods," you can get a clue as to the number and difficulty of questions to be asked in any given field. More questions, and hence broader coverage, would be included for those subjects which are more important in the work. Now weigh your strengths and weaknesses against the job requirements and prepare accordingly.

3) Determine the level of the position

Another way to tell how intensively you should prepare is to understand the level of the job for which you are applying. Is it the entering level? In other words, is this the position in which beginners in a field of work are hired? Or is it an intermediate or advanced level? Sometimes this is indicated by such words as "Junior" or "Senior" in the class title. Other jurisdictions use Roman numerals to designate the level – Clerk I, Clerk II, for example. The word "Supervisor" sometimes appears in the title. If the level is not indicated by the title, check the description of duties. Will you be working under very close supervision, or will you have responsibility for independent decisions in this work?

4) Choose appropriate study materials

Now that you know the subjects to be examined and the relative amount of each subject to be covered, you can choose suitable study materials. For beginning level jobs, or even advanced ones, if you have a pronounced weakness in some aspect of your training, read a modern, standard textbook in that field. Be sure it is up to date and has general coverage. Such books are normally available at your library, and the librarian will be glad to help you locate one. For entry-level positions, questions of appropriate difficulty are chosen – neither highly advanced questions, nor those too simple. Such questions require careful thought but not advanced training.

If the position for which you are applying is technical or advanced, you will read more advanced, specialized material. If you are already familiar with the basic principles of your field, elementary textbooks would waste your time. Concentrate on advanced textbooks and technical periodicals. Think through the concepts and review difficult problems in your field.

These are all general sources. You can get more ideas on your own initiative, following these leads. For example, training manuals and publications of the government agency which employs workers in your field can be useful, particularly for technical and professional positions. A letter or visit to the government department involved may result in more specific study suggestions, and certainly will provide you with a more definite idea of the exact nature of the position you are seeking.

III. KINDS OF TESTS

Tests are used for purposes other than measuring knowledge and ability to perform specified duties. For some positions, it is equally important to test ability to make adjustments to new situations or to profit from training. In others, basic mental abilities not dependent on information are essential. Questions which test these things may not appear as pertinent to the duties of the position as those which test for knowledge and information. Yet they are often highly important parts of a fair examination. For very general questions, it is almost impossible to help you direct your study efforts. What we can do is to point out some of the more common of these general abilities needed in public service positions and describe some typical questions.

1) General information

Broad, general information has been found useful for predicting job success in some kinds of work. This is tested in a variety of ways, from vocabulary lists to questions about current events. Basic background in some field of work, such as sociology or economics, may be sampled in a group of questions. Often these are principles which have become familiar to most persons through exposure rather than through formal training. It is difficult to advise you how to study for these questions; being alert to the world around you is our best suggestion.

2) Verbal ability

An example of an ability needed in many positions is verbal or language ability. Verbal ability is, in brief, the ability to use and understand words. Vocabulary and grammar tests are typical measures of this ability. Reading comprehension or paragraph interpretation questions are common in many kinds of civil service tests. You are given a paragraph of written material and asked to find its central meaning.

3) Numerical ability

Number skills can be tested by the familiar arithmetic problem, by checking paired lists of numbers to see which are alike and which are different, or by interpreting charts and graphs. In the latter test, a graph may be printed in the test booklet which you are asked to use as the basis for answering questions.

4) Observation

A popular test for law-enforcement positions is the observation test. A picture is shown to you for several minutes, then taken away. Questions about the picture test your ability to observe both details and larger elements.

5) Following directions

In many positions in the public service, the employee must be able to carry out written instructions dependably and accurately. You may be given a chart with several columns, each column listing a variety of information. The questions require you to carry out directions involving the information given in the chart.

6) Skills and aptitudes

Performance tests effectively measure some manual skills and aptitudes. When the skill is one in which you are trained, such as typing or shorthand, you can practice. These tests are often very much like those given in business school or high school courses. For many of the other skills and aptitudes, however, no short-time preparation can be made. Skills and abilities natural to you or that you have developed throughout your lifetime are being tested.

Many of the general questions just described provide all the data needed to answer the questions and ask you to use your reasoning ability to find the answers. Your best preparation for these tests, as well as for tests of facts and ideas, is to be at your physical and mental best. You, no doubt, have your own methods of getting into an exam-taking mood and keeping "in shape." The next section lists some ideas on this subject.

IV. KINDS OF QUESTIONS

Only rarely is the "essay" question, which you answer in narrative form, used in civil service tests. Civil service tests are usually of the short-answer type. Full instructions for answering these questions will be given to you at the examination. But in case this is your first experience with short-answer questions and separate answer sheets, here is what you need to know:

1) Multiple-choice Questions

Most popular of the short-answer questions is the "multiple choice" or "best answer" question. It can be used, for example, to test for factual knowledge, ability to solve problems or judgment in meeting situations found at work.

A multiple-choice question is normally one of three types—

- It can begin with an incomplete statement followed by several possible endings. You are to find the one ending which *best* completes the statement, although some of the others may not be entirely wrong.
- It can also be a complete statement in the form of a question which is answered by choosing one of the statements listed.
- It can be in the form of a problem – again you select the best answer.

Here is an example of a multiple-choice question with a discussion which should give you some clues as to the method for choosing the right answer:

When an employee has a complaint about his assignment, the action which will *best* help him overcome his difficulty is to
A. discuss his difficulty with his coworkers
B. take the problem to the head of the organization
C. take the problem to the person who gave him the assignment
D. say nothing to anyone about his complaint

In answering this question, you should study each of the choices to find which is best. Consider choice "A" – Certainly an employee may discuss his complaint with fellow employees, but no change or improvement can result, and the complaint remains unresolved. Choice "B" is a poor choice since the head of the organization probably does not know what assignment you have been given, and taking your problem to him is known as "going over the head" of the supervisor. The supervisor, or person who made the assignment, is the person who can clarify it or correct any injustice. Choice "C" is, therefore, correct. To say nothing, as in choice "D," is unwise. Supervisors have and interest in knowing the problems employees are facing, and the employee is seeking a solution to his problem.

2) True/False Questions

The "true/false" or "right/wrong" form of question is sometimes used. Here a complete statement is given. Your job is to decide whether the statement is right or wrong.

SAMPLE: A roaming cell-phone call to a nearby city costs less than a non-roaming call to a distant city.

This statement is wrong, or false, since roaming calls are more expensive.
This is not a complete list of all possible question forms, although most of the others are variations of these common types. You will always get complete directions for

answering questions. Be sure you understand *how* to mark your answers – ask questions until you do.

V. RECORDING YOUR ANSWERS

Computer terminals are used more and more today for many different kinds of exams.

For an examination with very few applicants, you may be told to record your answers in the test booklet itself. Separate answer sheets are much more common. If this separate answer sheet is to be scored by machine – and this is often the case – it is highly important that you mark your answers correctly in order to get credit.

An electronic scoring machine is often used in civil service offices because of the speed with which papers can be scored. Machine-scored answer sheets must be marked with a pencil, which will be given to you. This pencil has a high graphite content which responds to the electronic scoring machine. As a matter of fact, stray dots may register as answers, so do not let your pencil rest on the answer sheet while you are pondering the correct answer. Also, if your pencil lead breaks or is otherwise defective, ask for another.

Since the answer sheet will be dropped in a slot in the scoring machine, be careful not to bend the corners or get the paper crumpled.

The answer sheet normally has five vertical columns of numbers, with 30 numbers to a column. These numbers correspond to the question numbers in your test booklet. After each number, going across the page are four or five pairs of dotted lines. These short dotted lines have small letters or numbers above them. The first two pairs may also have a "T" or "F" above the letters. This indicates that the first two pairs only are to be used if the questions are of the true-false type. If the questions are multiple choice, disregard the "T" and "F" and pay attention only to the small letters or numbers.

Answer your questions in the manner of the sample that follows:

32. The largest city in the United States is
     A. Washington, D.C.
     B. New York City
     C. Chicago
     D. Detroit
     E. San Francisco

1) Choose the answer you think is best. (New York City is the largest, so "B" is correct.)
2) Find the row of dotted lines numbered the same as the question you are answering. (Find row number 32)
3) Find the pair of dotted lines corresponding to the answer. (Find the pair of lines under the mark "B.")
4) Make a solid black mark between the dotted lines.

VI. BEFORE THE TEST

Common sense will help you find procedures to follow to get ready for an examination. Too many of us, however, overlook these sensible measures. Indeed, nervousness and fatigue have been found to be the most serious reasons why applicants fail to do their best on civil service tests. Here is a list of reminders:

- Begin your preparation early – Don't wait until the last minute to go scurrying around for books and materials or to find out what the position is all about.
- Prepare continuously – An hour a night for a week is better than an all-night cram session. This has been definitely established. What is more, a night a week for a month will return better dividends than crowding your study into a shorter period of time.
- Locate the place of the exam – You have been sent a notice telling you when and where to report for the examination. If the location is in a different town or otherwise unfamiliar to you, it would be well to inquire the best route and learn something about the building.
- Relax the night before the test – Allow your mind to rest. Do not study at all that night. Plan some mild recreation or diversion; then go to bed early and get a good night's sleep.
- Get up early enough to make a leisurely trip to the place for the test – This way unforeseen events, traffic snarls, unfamiliar buildings, etc. will not upset you.
- Dress comfortably – A written test is not a fashion show. You will be known by number and not by name, so wear something comfortable.
- Leave excess paraphernalia at home – Shopping bags and odd bundles will get in your way. You need bring only the items mentioned in the official notice you received; usually everything you need is provided. Do not bring reference books to the exam. They will only confuse those last minutes and be taken away from you when in the test room.
- Arrive somewhat ahead of time – If because of transportation schedules you must get there very early, bring a newspaper or magazine to take your mind off yourself while waiting.
- Locate the examination room – When you have found the proper room, you will be directed to the seat or part of the room where you will sit. Sometimes you are given a sheet of instructions to read while you are waiting. Do not fill out any forms until you are told to do so; just read them and be prepared.
- Relax and prepare to listen to the instructions
- If you have any physical problem that may keep you from doing your best, be sure to tell the test administrator. If you are sick or in poor health, you really cannot do your best on the exam. You can come back and take the test some other time.

VII. AT THE TEST

The day of the test is here and you have the test booklet in your hand. The temptation to get going is very strong. Caution! There is more to success than knowing the right answers. You must know how to identify your papers and understand variations in the type of short-answer question used in this particular examination. Follow these suggestions for maximum results from your efforts:

1) Cooperate with the monitor

The test administrator has a duty to create a situation in which you can be as much at ease as possible. He will give instructions, tell you when to begin, check to see that you are marking your answer sheet correctly, and so on. He is not there to guard you, although he will see that your competitors do not take unfair advantage. He wants to help you do your best.

2) Listen to all instructions

Don't jump the gun! Wait until you understand all directions. In most civil service tests you get more time than you need to answer the questions. So don't be in a hurry. Read each word of instructions until you clearly understand the meaning. Study the examples, listen to all announcements and follow directions. Ask questions if you do not understand what to do.

3) Identify your papers

Civil service exams are usually identified by number only. You will be assigned a number; you must not put your name on your test papers. Be sure to copy your number correctly. Since more than one exam may be given, copy your exact examination title.

4) Plan your time

Unless you are told that a test is a "speed" or "rate of work" test, speed itself is usually not important. Time enough to answer all the questions will be provided, but this does not mean that you have all day. An overall time limit has been set. Divide the total time (in minutes) by the number of questions to determine the approximate time you have for each question.

5) Do not linger over difficult questions

If you come across a difficult question, mark it with a paper clip (useful to have along) and come back to it when you have been through the booklet. One caution if you do this – be sure to skip a number on your answer sheet as well. Check often to be sure that you have not lost your place and that you are marking in the row numbered the same as the question you are answering.

6) Read the questions

Be sure you know what the question asks! Many capable people are unsuccessful because they failed to *read* the questions correctly.

7) Answer all questions

Unless you have been instructed that a penalty will be deducted for incorrect answers, it is better to guess than to omit a question.

8) Speed tests

It is often better NOT to guess on speed tests. It has been found that on timed tests people are tempted to spend the last few seconds before time is called in marking answers at random – without even reading them – in the hope of picking up a few extra points. To discourage this practice, the instructions may warn you that your score will be "corrected" for guessing. That is, a penalty will be applied. The incorrect answers will be deducted from the correct ones, or some other penalty formula will be used.

9) Review your answers

If you finish before time is called, go back to the questions you guessed or omitted to give them further thought. Review other answers if you have time.

10) Return your test materials

If you are ready to leave before others have finished or time is called, take ALL your materials to the monitor and leave quietly. Never take any test material with you. The monitor can discover whose papers are not complete, and taking a test booklet may be grounds for disqualification.

VIII. EXAMINATION TECHNIQUES

1) Read the general instructions carefully. These are usually printed on the first page of the exam booklet. As a rule, these instructions refer to the timing of the examination; the fact that you should not start work until the signal and must stop work at a signal, etc. If there are any *special* instructions, such as a choice of questions to be answered, make sure that you note this instruction carefully.

2) When you are ready to start work on the examination, that is as soon as the signal has been given, read the instructions to each question booklet, underline any key words or phrases, such as *least, best, outline, describe* and the like. In this way you will tend to answer as requested rather than discover on reviewing your paper that you *listed without describing*, that you selected the *worst* choice rather than the *best* choice, etc.

3) If the examination is of the objective or multiple-choice type – that is, each question will also give a series of possible answers: A, B, C or D, and you are called upon to select the best answer and write the letter next to that answer on your answer paper – it is advisable to start answering each question in turn. There may be anywhere from 50 to 100 such questions in the three or four hours allotted and you can see how much time would be taken if you read through all the questions before beginning to answer any. Furthermore, if you come across a question or group of questions which you know would be difficult to answer, it would undoubtedly affect your handling of all the other questions.

4) If the examination is of the essay type and contains but a few questions, it is a moot point as to whether you should read all the questions before starting to answer any one. Of course, if you are given a choice – say five out of seven and the like – then it is essential to read all the questions so you can eliminate the two that are most difficult. If, however, you are asked to answer all the questions, there may be danger in trying to answer the easiest one first because you may find that you will spend too much time on it. The best technique is to answer the first question, then proceed to the second, etc.

5) Time your answers. Before the exam begins, write down the time it started, then add the time allowed for the examination and write down the time it must be completed, then divide the time available somewhat as follows:

- If 3-1/2 hours are allowed, that would be 210 minutes. If you have 80 objective-type questions, that would be an average of 2-1/2 minutes per question. Allow yourself no more than 2 minutes per question, or a total of 160 minutes, which will permit about 50 minutes to review.
- If for the time allotment of 210 minutes there are 7 essay questions to answer, that would average about 30 minutes a question. Give yourself only 25 minutes per question so that you have about 35 minutes to review.

6) The most important instruction is to *read each question* and make sure you know what is wanted. The second most important instruction is to *time yourself properly* so that you answer every question. The third most important instruction is to *answer every question*. Guess if you have to but include something for each question. Remember that you will receive no credit for a blank and will probably receive some credit if you write something in answer to an essay question. If you guess a letter – say "B" for a multiple-choice question – you may have guessed right. If you leave a blank as an answer to a multiple-choice question, the examiners may respect your feelings but it will not add a point to your score. Some exams may penalize you for wrong answers, so in such cases *only*, you may not want to guess unless you have some basis for your answer.

7) Suggestions
   a. Objective-type questions
      1. Examine the question booklet for proper sequence of pages and questions
      2. Read all instructions carefully
      3. Skip any question which seems too difficult; return to it after all other questions have been answered
      4. Apportion your time properly; do not spend too much time on any single question or group of questions
      5. Note and underline key words – *all, most, fewest, least, best, worst, same, opposite,* etc.
      6. Pay particular attention to negatives
      7. Note unusual option, e.g., unduly long, short, complex, different or similar in content to the body of the question
      8. Observe the use of "hedging" words – *probably, may, most likely,* etc.
      9. Make sure that your answer is put next to the same number as the question
      10. Do not second-guess unless you have good reason to believe the second answer is definitely more correct
      11. Cross out original answer if you decide another answer is more accurate; do not erase until you are ready to hand your paper in
      12. Answer all questions; guess unless instructed otherwise
      13. Leave time for review

   b. Essay questions
      1. Read each question carefully
      2. Determine exactly what is wanted. Underline key words or phrases.
      3. Decide on outline or paragraph answer

4. Include many different points and elements unless asked to develop any one or two points or elements
5. Show impartiality by giving pros and cons unless directed to select one side only
6. Make and write down any assumptions you find necessary to answer the questions
7. Watch your English, grammar, punctuation and choice of words
8. Time your answers; don't crowd material

8) Answering the essay question

Most essay questions can be answered by framing the specific response around several key words or ideas. Here are a few such key words or ideas:

M's: manpower, materials, methods, money, management
P's: purpose, program, policy, plan, procedure, practice, problems, pitfalls, personnel, public relations
   a. Six basic steps in handling problems:
      1. Preliminary plan and background development
      2. Collect information, data and facts
      3. Analyze and interpret information, data and facts
      4. Analyze and develop solutions as well as make recommendations
      5. Prepare report and sell recommendations
      6. Install recommendations and follow up effectiveness

   b. Pitfalls to avoid
      1. *Taking things for granted* – A statement of the situation does not necessarily imply that each of the elements is necessarily true; for example, a complaint may be invalid and biased so that all that can be taken for granted is that a complaint has been registered
      2. *Considering only one side of a situation* – Wherever possible, indicate several alternatives and then point out the reasons you selected the best one
      3. *Failing to indicate follow up* – Whenever your answer indicates action on your part, make certain that you will take proper follow-up action to see how successful your recommendations, procedures or actions turn out to be
      4. *Taking too long in answering any single question* – Remember to time your answers properly

IX. AFTER THE TEST

Scoring procedures differ in detail among civil service jurisdictions although the general principles are the same. Whether the papers are hand-scored or graded by machine we have described, they are nearly always graded by number. That is, the person who marks the paper knows only the number – never the name – of the applicant. Not until all the papers have been graded will they be matched with names. If other tests, such as training and experience or oral interview ratings have been given, scores will be combined. Different parts of the examination usually have different weights. For example, the written test might count 60 percent of the final grade, and a rating of training and experience 40 percent. In many jurisdictions, veterans will have a certain number of points added to their grades.

After the final grade has been determined, the names are placed in grade order and an eligible list is established. There are various methods for resolving ties between those who get the same final grade – probably the most common is to place first the name of the person whose application was received first. Job offers are made from the eligible list in the order the names appear on it. You will be notified of your grade and your rank as soon as all these computations have been made. This will be done as rapidly as possible.

People who are found to meet the requirements in the announcement are called "eligibles." Their names are put on a list of eligible candidates. An eligible's chances of getting a job depend on how high he stands on this list and how fast agencies are filling jobs from the list.

When a job is to be filled from a list of eligibles, the agency asks for the names of people on the list of eligibles for that job. When the civil service commission receives this request, it sends to the agency the names of the three people highest on this list. Or, if the job to be filled has specialized requirements, the office sends the agency the names of the top three persons who meet these requirements from the general list.

The appointing officer makes a choice from among the three people whose names were sent to him. If the selected person accepts the appointment, the names of the others are put back on the list to be considered for future openings.

That is the rule in hiring from all kinds of eligible lists, whether they are for typist, carpenter, chemist, or something else. For every vacancy, the appointing officer has his choice of any one of the top three eligibles on the list. This explains why the person whose name is on top of the list sometimes does not get an appointment when some of tho persons lower on the list do. If the appointing officer chooses the second or third eligible, the No. 1 eligible does not get a job at once, but stays on the list until he is appointed or the list is terminated.

X. HOW TO PASS THE INTERVIEW TEST

The examination for which you applied requires an oral interview test. You have already taken the written test and you are now being called for the interview test – the final part of the formal examination.

You may think that it is not possible to prepare for an interview test and that there are no procedures to follow during an interview. Our purpose is to point out some things you can do in advance that will help you and some good rules to follow and pitfalls to avoid while you are being interviewed.

What is an interview supposed to test?
The written examination is designed to test the technical knowledge and competence of the candidate; the oral is designed to evaluate intangible qualities, not readily measured otherwise, and to establish a list showing the relative fitness of each candidate – as measured against his competitors – for the position sought. Scoring is not on the basis of "right" and "wrong," but on a sliding scale of values ranging from "not passable" to "outstanding." As a matter of fact, it is possible to achieve a relatively low score without a single "incorrect" answer because of evident weakness in the qualities being measured.

Occasionally, an examination may consist entirely of an oral test – either an individual or a group oral. In such cases, information is sought concerning the technical knowledges and abilities of the candidate, since there has been no written examination for this purpose. More commonly, however, an oral test is used to supplement a written examination.

Who conducts interviews?

The composition of oral boards varies among different jurisdictions. In nearly all, a representative of the personnel department serves as chairman. One of the members of the board may be a representative of the department in which the candidate would work. In some cases, "outside experts" are used, and, frequently, a businessman or some other representative of the general public is asked to serve. Labor and management or other special groups may be represented. The aim is to secure the services of experts in the appropriate field.

However the board is composed, it is a good idea (and not at all improper or unethical) to ascertain in advance of the interview who the members are and what groups they represent. When you are introduced to them, you will have some idea of their backgrounds and interests, and at least you will not stutter and stammer over their names.

What should be done before the interview?

While knowledge about the board members is useful and takes some of the surprise element out of the interview, there is other preparation which is more substantive. It *is* possible to prepare for an oral interview – in several ways:

1) Keep a copy of your application and review it carefully before the interview

This may be the only document before the oral board, and the starting point of the interview. Know what education and experience you have listed there, and the sequence and dates of all of it. Sometimes the board will ask you to review the highlights of your experience for them; you should not have to hem and haw doing it.

2) Study the class specification and the examination announcement

Usually, the oral board has one or both of these to guide them. The qualities, characteristics or knowledges required by the position sought are stated in these documents. They offer valuable clues as to the nature of the oral interview. For example, if the job involves supervisory responsibilities, the announcement will usually indicate that knowledge of modern supervisory methods and the qualifications of the candidate as a supervisor will be tested. If so, you can expect such questions, frequently in the form of a hypothetical situation which you are expected to solve. NEVER go into an oral without knowledge of the duties and responsibilities of the job you seek.

3) Think through each qualification required

Try to visualize the kind of questions you would ask if you were a board member. How well could you answer them? Try especially to appraise your own knowledge and background in each area, *measured against the job sought*, and identify any areas in which you are weak. Be critical and realistic – do not flatter yourself.

4) Do some general reading in areas in which you feel you may be weak

For example, if the job involves supervision and your past experience has NOT, some general reading in supervisory methods and practices, particularly in the field of human relations, might be useful. Do NOT study agency procedures or detailed manuals. The oral board will be testing your understanding and capacity, not your memory.

5) Get a good night's sleep and watch your general health and mental attitude

You will want a clear head at the interview. Take care of a cold or any other minor ailment, and of course, no hangovers.

What should be done on the day of the interview?

Now comes the day of the interview itself. Give yourself plenty of time to get there. Plan to arrive somewhat ahead of the scheduled time, particularly if your appointment is in the fore part of the day. If a previous candidate fails to appear, the board might be ready for you a bit early. By early afternoon an oral board is almost invariably behind schedule if there are many candidates, and you may have to wait. Take along a book or magazine to read, or your application to review, but leave any extraneous material in the waiting room when you go in for your interview. In any event, relax and compose yourself.

The matter of dress is important. The board is forming impressions about you – from your experience, your manners, your attitude, and your appearance. Give your personal appearance careful attention. Dress your best, but not your flashiest. Choose conservative, appropriate clothing, and be sure it is immaculate. This is a business interview, and your appearance should indicate that you regard it as such. Besides, being well groomed and properly dressed will help boost your confidence.

Sooner or later, someone will call your name and escort you into the interview room. *This is it.* From here on you are on your own. It is too late for any more preparation. But remember, you asked for this opportunity to prove your fitness, and you are here because your request was granted.

What happens when you go in?

The usual sequence of events will be as follows: The clerk (who is often the board stenographer) will introduce you to the chairman of the oral board, who will introduce you to the other members of the board. Acknowledge the introductions before you sit down. Do not be surprised if you find a microphone facing you or a stenotypist sitting by. Oral interviews are usually recorded in the event of an appeal or other review.

Usually the chairman of the board will open the interview by reviewing the highlights of your education and work experience from your application – primarily for the benefit of the other members of the board, as well as to get the material into the record. Do not interrupt or comment unless there is an error or significant misinterpretation; if that is the case, do not hesitate. But do not quibble about insignificant matters. Also, he will usually ask you some question about your education, experience or your present job – partly to get you to start talking and to establish the interviewing "rapport." He may start the actual questioning, or turn it over to one of the other members. Frequently, each member undertakes the questioning on a particular area, one in which he is perhaps most competent, so you can expect each member to participate in the examination. Because time is limited, you may also expect some rather abrupt switches in the direction the questioning takes, so do not be upset by it. Normally, a board member will not pursue a single line of questioning unless he discovers a particular strength or weakness.

After each member has participated, the chairman will usually ask whether any member has any further questions, then will ask you if you have anything you wish to add. Unless you are expecting this question, it may floor you. Worse, it may start you off on an extended, extemporaneous speech. The board is not usually seeking more information. The question is principally to offer you a last opportunity to present further qualifications or to indicate that you have nothing to add. So, if you feel that a significant qualification or characteristic has been overlooked, it is proper to point it out in a sentence or so. Do not compliment the board on the thoroughness of their examination – they have been sketchy, and you know it. If you wish, merely say, "No thank you, I have nothing further to add." This is a point where you can "talk yourself out" of a good impression or fail to present an important bit of information. Remember, *you close the interview yourself.*

The chairman will then say, "That is all, Mr. _____, thank you." Do not be startled; the interview is over, and quicker than you think. Thank him, gather your belongings and take your leave. Save your sigh of relief for the other side of the door.

How to put your best foot forward

Throughout this entire process, you may feel that the board individually and collectively is trying to pierce your defenses, seek out your hidden weaknesses and embarrass and confuse you. Actually, this is not true. They are obliged to make an appraisal of your qualifications for the job you are seeking, and they want to see you in your best light. Remember, they must interview all candidates and a non-cooperative candidate may become a failure in spite of their best efforts to bring out his qualifications. Here are 15 suggestions that will help you:

1) Be natural – Keep your attitude confident, not cocky

If you are not confident that you can do the job, do not expect the board to be. Do not apologize for your weaknesses, try to bring out your strong points. The board is interested in a positive, not negative, presentation. Cockiness will antagonize any board member and make him wonder if you are covering up a weakness by a false show of strength.

2) Get comfortable, but don't lounge or sprawl

Sit erectly but not stiffly. A careless posture may lead the board to conclude that you are careless in other things, or at least that you are not impressed by the importance of the occasion. Either conclusion is natural, even if incorrect. Do not fuss with your clothing, a pencil or an ashtray. Your hands may occasionally be useful to emphasize a point; do not let them become a point of distraction.

3) Do not wisecrack or make small talk

This is a serious situation, and your attitude should show that you consider it as such. Further, the time of the board is limited – they do not want to waste it, and neither should you.

4) Do not exaggerate your experience or abilities

In the first place, from information in the application or other interviews and sources, the board may know more about you than you think. Secondly, you probably will not get away with it. An experienced board is rather adept at spotting such a situation, so do not take the chance.

5) If you know a board member, do not make a point of it, yet do not hide it

Certainly you are not fooling him, and probably not the other members of the board. Do not try to take advantage of your acquaintanceship – it will probably do you little good.

6) Do not dominate the interview

Let the board do that. They will give you the clues – do not assume that you have to do all the talking. Realize that the board has a number of questions to ask you, and do not try to take up all the interview time by showing off your extensive knowledge of the answer to the first one.

7) Be attentive

You only have 20 minutes or so, and you should keep your attention at its sharpest throughout. When a member is addressing a problem or question to you, give him your undivided attention. Address your reply principally to him, but do not exclude the other board members.

8) Do not interrupt

A board member may be stating a problem for you to analyze. He will ask you a question when the time comes. Let him state the problem, and wait for the question.

9) Make sure you understand the question

Do not try to answer until you are sure what the question is. If it is not clear, restate it in your own words or ask the board member to clarify it for you. However, do not haggle about minor elements.

10) Reply promptly but not hastily

A common entry on oral board rating sheets is "candidate responded readily," or "candidate hesitated in replies." Respond as promptly and quickly as you can, but do not jump to a hasty, ill-considered answer.

11) Do not be peremptory in your answers

A brief answer is proper – but do not fire your answer back. That is a losing game from your point of view. The board member can probably ask questions much faster than you can answer them.

12) Do not try to create the answer you think the board member wants

He is interested in what kind of mind you have and how it works – not in playing games. Furthermore, he can usually spot this practice and will actually grade you down on it.

13) Do not switch sides in your reply merely to agree with a board member

Frequently, a member will take a contrary position merely to draw you out and to see if you are willing and able to defend your point of view. Do not start a debate, yet do not surrender a good position. If a position is worth taking, it is worth defending.

14) Do not be afraid to admit an error in judgment if you are shown to be wrong

  The board knows that you are forced to reply without any opportunity for careful consideration. Your answer may be demonstrably wrong. If so, admit it and get on with the interview.

15) Do not dwell at length on your present job

  The opening question may relate to your present assignment. Answer the question but do not go into an extended discussion. You are being examined for a *new* job, not your present one. As a matter of fact, try to phrase ALL your answers in terms of the job for which you are being examined.

Basis of Rating

  Probably you will forget most of these "do's" and "don'ts" when you walk into the oral interview room. Even remembering them all will not ensure you a passing grade. Perhaps you did not have the qualifications in the first place. But remembering them will help you to put your best foot forward, without treading on the toes of the board members.

  Rumor and popular opinion to the contrary notwithstanding, an oral board wants you to make the best appearance possible. They know you are under pressure – but they also want to see how you respond to it as a guide to what your reaction would be under the pressures of the job you seek. They will be influenced by the degree of poise you display, the personal traits you show and the manner in which you respond.

ABOUT THIS BOOK

  This book contains tests divided into Examination Sections. Go through each test, answering every question in the margin. At the end of each test look at the answer key and check your answers. On the ones you got wrong, look at the right answer choice and learn. Do not fill in the answers first. Do not memorize the questions and answers, but understand the answer and principles involved. On your test, the questions will likely be different from the samples. Questions are changed and new ones added. If you understand these past questions you should have success with any changes that arise. Tests may consist of several types of questions. We have additional books on each subject should more study be advisable or necessary for you. Finally, the more you study, the better prepared you will be. This book is intended to be the last thing you study before you walk into the examination room. Prior study of relevant texts is also recommended. NLC publishes some of these in our Fundamental Series. Knowledge and good sense are important factors in passing your exam. Good luck also helps. So now study this Passbook, absorb the material contained within and take that knowledge into the examination. Then do your best to pass that exam.

―――――

EXAMINATION SECTION

EXAMINATION SECTION
TEST 1

DIRECTIONS: Each question or incomplete statement is followed by several suggested answers or completions. Select the one the BEST answers the question or completes the statement. *PRINT THE LETTER OF THE CORRECT ANSWER IN THE SPACE AT THE RIGHT.*

1. The type of property/evidence that is most likely to involve the "two person" rule for handling is

    A. currency
    B. firearms
    C. flammable material
    D. biohazardous material

1.____

2. An affidavit is most likely to be required in a record for

    A. found property
    B. property seized by search warrant
    C. property held for safekeeping
    D. recovered property

2.____

3. "Temporary storage" refers to the

    A. gap between the time the employee who seized the property leaves it at the station, and the time that it is actually received by a property room employee
    B. gap between the time an item is signed out for disposition and the time that it is actually disposed of
    C. time during which non-evidentiary property is placed in the custody of a law enforcement agency for temporary protection on behalf of the owner
    D. span of any applicable statute of limitations that impacts the amount of time an item is required to remain in custody

3.____

4. When storing audio- or videotapes and computer disks, it's important to remember that air, heat, moisture, and magnetism may deteriorate these items within

    A. 6-8 months
    B. 1-2 years
    C. 5-6 years
    D. 10-12 years

4.____

5. A standard property/evidence record should include
    I. date/time collected/submitted
    II. special instructions
    III. chain of custody
    IV. storage location

    A. I only
    B. I and III
    C. I, II and III
    D. I, II, III and IV

5.____

6. Biological materials must be in a sealed/container or bag   6._____

    A. if they are in transit
    B. only if they are to be used as evidence
    C. at all times
    D. if they are going to be tested again

7. Ideally, the outdoor "bulk area" of a property/evidence section would contain   7._____

    I. automobiles
    II. flammable materials
    III. firearms
    IV. bicycles

    A. I only
    B. I and IV
    C. I, II and IV
    D. I, II, III and IV

8. Materials and supplies used by the property/evidence section should be kept in the   8._____

    A. evidence review room
    B. general property/evidence storage area
    C. departmental office
    D. storage area separate from the entire section's facilities

9. Generally, inventories of property/evidence sections should be completed   9._____

    A. every three months
    B. every six months
    C. annually
    D. every two years

10. During an inventory, a property specialist comes across an item on the shelf that is not documented anywhere in department records. The item should be listed on a(n)   10._____

    A. found property report
    B. disposition form
    C. unable to locate file
    D. right of refusal

11. When fingerprints on an item may be relevant and are a possibility, the item should be   11._____

    A. dusted for prints
    B. stored at room temperature
    C. frozen
    D. refrigerated

12. Guidelines for firearms storage include   12._____

    I. room should be alarmed independent of regular intrusion alarm system
    II. weapons should be secured in a manner that makes them impossible to fire
    III. weapons recovered from an underwater location should be cleaned
    IV. generally, firearms to be submitted for forensic processing should be packaged in an airtight container

A. I and II
B. II only
C. I, II and III
D. I, II, III and IV

13. What is the term for non-evidentiary property which, after coming into the custody of a   13.____
    law enforcement agency, has been determined to be lost or abandoned and is not known
    or suspected to be connected with any criminal offense?

    A. Property for safekeeping
    B. Found property
    C. Property for disposition
    D. Recovered property

14. Within a property/evidence section, narcotics which are most susceptible to theft from   14.____
    within the department are those which have

    A. just been signed off for disposition
    B. not yet been entered into evidence
    C. just been entered into evidence
    D. logged and stored indefinitely

15. Liquid items of biological samples, such as tubes of blood, that are meant to be tested   15.____
    again should be

    A. dried first, then stored at room temperature
    B. stored in refrigerator temperatures of 36-50 degrees Fahrenheit
    C. stored in freezer temperatures of below 32 degrees Fahrenheit
    D. vacuum-sealed, then stored at room temperature

16. For the handling, storage, and maintenance of high-profile items (narcotics, biological   16.____
    materials, firearms, currency, etc.), guidelines include each of the following, EXCEPT

    A. vaults should be constructed of concrete or block
    B. storage should be an exception to the overall property room location and scheme
    C. locking mechanisms should be designed so that two people are needed for entry
    D. alarm systems should consist of an intrusion alarm with door contacts and motion
       sensors

17. From the property specialist's standpoint, which of the following types of narcotics has   17.____
    different packaging requirements from most other kinds of drugs?

    A. partially processed methamphetamine
    B. cocaine
    C. green marijuana
    D. PCP

18. The original documentation of a property/evidence section inventory would be BEST   18.____
    kept

    A. with the records of the property/evidence section records
    B. with the agency's records bureau
    C. in a high-security area such as the firearms cabinet
    D. in the property supervisor/captain's office

19. Evidence stored with a property/evidence section may be disposed of if
     I.   it poses a physical hazard
    II.   it is found property with unknown origins
   III.   the case is subject to DA refiling
   IV.   the case has multiple defendants

   A.   I only
   B.   I and III
   C.   III only
   D.   III and IV

19.____

20. Any property or evidence submitted to the property/evidence section should have an envelope, tag, or label affixed to it, usually corresponding with the _____ listed on the record.

   A.   submitting officer
   B.   case number
   C.   classification
   D.   item number

20.____

21. Which of the following is a guideline for the storage of computers?

   A.   Disks and other storage media should be detached and stored separately.
   B.   They should be stored in a covered outdoor bulk area.
   C.   Towers should be stored in the position they were used in.
   D.   They should be tightly sealed in metal containers.

21.____

22. Most appropriately, a departmental review of property/evidence for disposition would consist of

   A.   basing disposition of statutes of limitations
   B.   a complete inventory every 6 months-1 year
   C.   a review of all criminal cases every 6 months-1 year
   D.   an external audit of the efficiency with which space is being used

22.____

23. A standard currency envelope should contain each of the following, EXCEPT a

   A.   space for witness verification
   B.   space for the initials and the ID number of the person seizing and counting the currency
   C.   line for the name of additional owners/suspects whose cash is also included in the envelope
   D.   register of currency and coins in the envelope, by denomination

23.____

24. Guidelines for recording and storing narcotics include
     I.   weights should be specified with (gross total weight) or without (net weight) packaging material
    II.   after sealing the package, the only staff who should be authorized to re-open it are lab staff
   III.   most narcotics should be stored in a heat-sealed plastic bag
   IV.   scales used should be recalibrated at least twice a year

   A.   I only
   B.   I and II

24.____

C. I, II and IV
D. I, II, III and IV

25. It's important to note, prior to disposition, that _____ can be considered hazardous   25._____
     waste because of the chemicals used to manufacture them.

A. television sets
B. computer circuit boards
C. computer hard drives
D. firearms

_____

KEY (CORRECT ANSWERS)

1.	A		11.	B
2.	A		12.	A
3.	A		13.	B
4.	C		14.	A
5.	D		15.	B
6.	A		16.	B
7.	C		17.	C
8.	D		18.	B
9.	C		19.	A
10.	A		20.	D

21.	C
22.	C
23.	C
24.	D
25.	B

_____

TEST 2

Each question or incomplete statement is followed by several suggested answers or completions. Select the one the BEST answers the question or completes the statement. *PRINT THE LETTER OF THE CORRECT ANSWER IN THE SPACE AT THE RIGHT.*

1. The best method for marking a firearm is to attach an identification tag to the 1.____

    A. hammer
    B. checkered portion of the grip
    C. barrel
    D. trigger guard

2. "Chain of custody" of an item of evidence is usually considered to have been initiated by the 2.____

    A. property/evidence specialist
    B. original owner
    C. involved party
    D. recovering/reporting officer

3. Generally, the last item to appear on a standard property/evidence record is 3.____

    A. disposition
    B. involved party name
    C. storage location
    D. submitting officer/employee

4. The primary purpose of a property/evidence room inventory is to 4.____

    A. ensure continuity of custody
    B. provide quality control for departmental operations
    C. account for every single item of property
    D. streamline processes

5. The "Big Three" of in-custody property, which require extra protection, security, and handling precautions, include each of the following, EXCEPT 5.____

    A. firearms
    B. biohazardous materials
    C. narcotics
    D. currency

6. Probably the single most important factor in making the operation of a property/evidence section more efficient is 6.____

    A. commingling of different types of evidence in the same area
    B. packaging standards
    C. statutes of limitations
    D. transfer protocols

7. Bloody evidence, or evidence contaminated with other body fluids, should be dried in a controlled, secure environment. Once dried, the items are best stored in 7.____

A. airtight plastic
B. paper bags
C. the open air
D. tightly-wrapped foil

8. If not a separate department within a law enforcement agency, the property/evidence function is most appropriately placed under the authority of   8.____

A. support services/administration
B. investigations division
C. property crimes division
D. uniform division

9. A submitting officer presents a sealed currency envelope to a property specialist without an accompanying verification signature. The property specialist should   9.____

A. ask the officer to list the currency and coin by denomination
B. open the envelope and count the currency in order to provide corroboration
C. immediately transfer the currency to the general fund or finance department
D. exercise right of refusal

10. Containers used to store audio- or videotapes or computer disks should be each of the following, EXCEPT   10.____

A. airtight
B. water-tight
C. metallic
D. non-static

11. Guidelines for conducting property/evidence section inventories include   11.____
   I.   begin random inventories only from easy-to-describe locations
   II. if possible, conduct the inventory from paper to shelf
   III. if possible, avoid breaking evidence seals to verify contents
   IV. inventories of narcotics signed out for destruction should include random testing to determine purity

A. I only
B. I, III and IV
C. II and III
D. III and IV

12. When fireworks that have been stored with a property/evidence section are ready for disposal, the most appropriate agency for the job is the   12.____

A. law enforcement agency that held them
B. Federal Bureau of Investigation
C. local fire department
D. federal ATF bureau

13. Guidelines for the storage of flammable materials include   13.____
   I.   fire extinguishers or sprinkler systems should be available in the storage area
   II. storage in a metal container

    III.   storage in an airtight container
    IV.   if possible, storage outside the property room

    A. I only
    B. I and II
    C. I, II and III
    D. I, II, III and IV

14. During an inventory, the seal on an envelope is broken. Which of the following is true?   14.____

    A. Any property contained within the envelope must now be destroyed.
    B. The contents must be verified and documented prior to resealing.
    C. The contents of the envelope are no longer admissible as evidence.
    D. The replacement seal does not require a witness.

15. For narcotic evidence not taken into custody or destroyed at the scene, the recommended documentation method is   15.____

    A. photographs taken prior to destruction
    B. small (.5 mg) samples taken and filed into envelopes
    C. an affidavit filed by the collecting officer and witnessed by the property specialist as to the type and amount of substance
    D. a simple written description filed with property/evidence section records

16. Unless disposal release is explicitly ordered, property/evidence from _____ should be held indefinitely.   16.____
    I.   falsification of public documents
    II.   embezzlement of public funds
    III.   felony sexual offenses
    IV.   capital homicides

    A. I and II
    B. I, II and IV
    C. III and IV
    D. IV only

17. To balance a desire to maximize a return on budgetary resources with the likelihood of future obsolescence, a property/evidence section should keep a minimum of about _____'s worth of forms (records, transfers, etc.) in stock.   17.____

    A. 3 months
    B. 6 months
    C. 1 year
    D. 3 years

18. Which of the following is LEAST likely to be accepted into a property room as evidence for storage?   18.____

    A. Bicycle
    B. Hypodermic syringe
    C. Currency
    D. Alcoholic beverage container

19. Bar coding systems, if used in a property/evidence records system, should allow for   19.____
      I.   password security
      II.   validation against the host system
      III.   on-demand label printing
      IV.   data collection programs for portable terminals

    A.   I and II
    B.   II only
    C.   II, III and IV
    D.   I, II, III and IV

20. The most efficient and trouble-free way to inventory a property/ evidence section is to   20.____

    A.   inventory different types of items at specific times of the year
    B.   work only from active case files
    C.   perform the inventory all at once at the beginning of each year
    D.   consult records only, without looking through individual items

21. When planning or adjusting the layout for a property/evidence storage area, it's important   21.____
to remember that property for safekeeping

    A.   should be commingled with non-quarantined evidence
    B.   requires its own separate ventilation system
    C.   needs quick, open access and close proximity to the public counter
    D.   should be placed on special shelving

22. The most significant factor influencing a property specialist's decision to dispose of prop-   22.____
erty or evidence is likely to be

    A.   civil litigation risk
    B.   auditing/inventory time
    C.   space limitations
    D.   increasing potential for misplacing items

23. Transfer forms used by property/evidence sections should NOT   23.____

    A.   include a brief description
    B.   indicate to whom the property was released
    C.   name the intended destination
    D.   be fastened to the original paperwork while in transit

24. Biological materials that are dried stains, and that are meant to be tested again, should   24.____
be stored

    A.   in the open air
    B.   in an airtight container at room temperature
    C.   in refrigerator temperatures of 36-50 degrees Fahrenheit
    D.   in freezer temperatures of below 32 degrees Fahrenheit

25. A law enforcement agency has discovered an item of found property in its storage facility,   25.____
and a quick search reveals the owner's identity. Which of the following may be true?
      I.   The law enforcement agency is not required to notify the owner.
      II.   The owner usually has 90 days after the receipt of the property by the
        agency to prove his ownership and reclaim the property.

III. The item has become the property of the law enforcement agency.
IV. The agency is authorized to require payment by the owner of a reasonable charge to defray the cost of storage and care of the property.

A. I and II
B. I, II and III
C. II and IV
D. I, II, III and IV

KEY (CORRECT ANSWERS)

1.	D		11.	B
2.	D		12.	C
3.	A		13.	D
4.	A		14.	B
5.	B		15.	A
6.	B		16.	B
7.	B		17.	C
8.	A		18.	B
9.	D		19.	D
10.	C		20.	A

21.	C
22.	C
23.	D
24.	D
25.	C

EXAMINATION SECTION
TEST 1

DIRECTIONS: Each question or incomplete statement is followed by several suggested answers or completions. Select the one that BEST answers the question or completes the statement. *PRINT THE LETTER OF THE CORRECT ANSWER IN THE SPACE AT THE RIGHT.*

Questions 1-8.

DIRECTIONS: Each of Questions 1 through 8 consists of a statement which contains a word (one of those underlined) that is either incorrectly used because it is not in keeping with the meaning the quotation is evidently intended to convey or is misspelled. There is only one INCORRECT word in each quotation. Of the four underlined words, determine if the first one should be replaced by the word lettered A, the second replaced by the word lettered B, the third replaced by the word lettered C, or the fourth replaced by the word lettered D. Print the letter of the replacement word you have selected in the space at the right.

1. Whether one depends on <u>fluorescent</u> or artificial light or both, adequate <u>standards</u> should be <u>maintained</u> by means of <u>systematic</u> tests.

   A. natural   B. safeguards
   C. established   D. routine

   1.____

2. A policeman has to be <u>prepared</u> to assume his <u>knowledge</u> as a social <u>scientist</u> in the <u>community</u>.

   A. forced   B. role
   C. philosopher   D. street

   2.____

3. It is <u>practically</u> impossible to <u>indicate</u> whether a sentence is <u>too</u> long simply by <u>measuring</u> its length.

   A. almost   B. tell   C. very   D. guessing

   3.____

4. Strong <u>leaders</u> are <u>required</u> to organize a community for delinquency prevention and for <u>dissemination</u> of organized <u>crime</u> and drug addiction.

   A. tactics   B. important   C. control   D. meetings

   4.____

5. The <u>demonstrators</u>, who were taken to the Criminal Courts building in <u>Manhattan</u> (because it was large enough to <u>accommodate</u> them), contended that the arrests were <u>unwarrented</u>.

   A. exhibitors   B. legirons
   C. adjudicate   D. unwarranted

   5.____

6. They were <u>guaranteed</u> a calm <u>atmosphere,</u> free from <u>harrassment</u>, which would be conducive to quiet consideration of the <u>indictments</u>.

   A. guarenteed   B. atmospher
   C. harassment   D. inditements

   6.____

7. The <u>alleged</u> killer was <u>occasionally</u> <u>permitted</u> to <u>excercise</u> in the corridor.　　　　7.___

    A. alledged   B. ocasionally
    C. permited   D. exercise

8. Defense <u>counsel</u> stated, in <u>affect,</u> that <u>their</u> conduct was <u>permissible</u> under the First   8.___
Amendment.

    A. council   B. effect
    C. there   D. permissable

Questions 9-12.

DIRECTIONS: Each of the two sentences in Questions 9 through 12 may be correct or may contain errors in punctuation, capitalization, or grammar. If there is an error only in sentence I, mark your answer A. If there is an error only in sentence II, mark your answer B. If there is an error in both sentence I and sentence II, mark your answer C. If both sentence I and sentence II are correct, mark your answer D.

9.   I. It is very annoying to have a pencil sharpener, which is not in working order.   9.___
    II. Patrolman Blake checked the door of Joe's Restaurant and found that the lock has been jammed.

10.   I. When you are studying a good textbook is important.   10.___
    II. He said he would divide the money equally between you and me.

11.   I. Since he went on the city council a year ago, one of his primary concerns has been   11.___
safety in the streets.
    II. After waiting in the doorway for about 15 minutes, a black sedan appeared.

12.   I. The question is, "What is the difference between a lawful and an unlawful demon-   12.___
stration?"
    II. The captain assigned two detectives, John and I, to the investigation.

Questions 13-14.

DIRECTIONS: In each of Questions 13 and 14, the four sentences are from a paragraph in a report. They are not in the right order. Which of the following arrangements is the BEST one?

13.   I. Most organizations favor one of the types but always include the others to a   13.___
lesser degree.
    II. However, we can detect a definite trend toward greater use of symbolic control.
    III. We suggest that our local police agencies are today primarily utilizing material control.
    IV. Control can be classified into three types: physical, material, and symbolic
The CORRECT answer is:

    A. IV, II, III, I   B. II, I, IV, III
    C. III, IV, II, I   D. IV, I, III, II

14.   I.   They can and do take advantage of ancient political and geographical boundaries,   14.____
           which often give them sanctuary from effective police activity.
      II. This country is essentially a country of small police forces, each operating inde-
           pendently within the limits of its jurisdiction.
      III. The boundaries that define and limit police operations do not hinder the move-
           ment of criminals, of course.
      IV. The machinery of law enforcement in America is fragmented, complicated, and
           frequently overlapping.
      The CORRECT answer is:

      A.   III, I, II, IV   B.   II, IV, I, III
      C.   IV, II, III, I   D.   IV, III, II, I

15.   Generally, the frequency with which reports are to be submitted or the length of the inter-   15.____
      val which they cover should depend MAINLY on the

      A.   amount of time needed to prepare the reports
      B.   degree of comprehensiveness required in the reports
      C.   availability of the data to be included in the reports
      D.   extent of the variations in the data with the passage of time

16.   Suppose you have to write a report on a serious infraction of rules by one of the Police   16.____
      Administrative Aides you supervise. The circumstances in which the infraction occurred
      are quite complicated. The BEST way to organize this report would be to

      A.   give all points equal emphasis throughout the report
      B.   include more than one point in a paragraph only if necessary to equalize the size of
           paragraphs
      C.   place the least important points before the most important points
      D.   present each significant point in a separate paragraph t

17.   Suppose that police expenses in the city in a certain year amounted to 7.5% of total   17.____
      expenses.
      In indicating this percentage on a *pie* or circular chart, which is 360, the size of the
      angle between the two radiuses would be MOST NEARLY

      A.   3.7   B.   7.5   C.   27   D.   54

18.   Suppose that in police precinct A, where there are 4180 children, 627 children entered a   18.____
      contest sponsored by the Police Community Relations Bureau. In precinct B, where there
      were 7840 children, 1960 children entered the contest. The total percentage of all chil-
      dren in both precincts who entered the contest amounted to MOST NEARLY

      A.   19.5%   B.   20%   C.   21.5%   D.   22.5%

19.   If Circle A represents Police Administrative Aides (PAA's) who   19.____
      scored above 85 on a PAA test and Circle B represents PAA's
      who scored above 85 on a Senior PAA test, then the diagram
      at the right means that

A. no PAA who scored above 85 on a PAA test scored above 85 on the Senior PAA test
B. the majority of PAA's who scored above 85 on a PAA test scored above 85 on the Senior PAA test
C. there were some PAA's who did not take the Senior PAA test
D. some PAA's who scored above 85 on a PAA test scored above 85 on the Senior PAA test

20. Suppose that in 1844 the city had a population of 550,000 and a police force of 200, and that in 1982 the city had a population of 8,000,000 and a police force of 32,000. If the ratio of police to population in 1982 is compared with the same ratio in 1844, what is the resulting relationship of the 1982 ratio to the 1844 ratio?   20.____

   A. 160:11   B. 160:1   C. 16:1   D. 11:1

Questions 21-24.

DIRECTIONS: Questions 21 through 24 are to be answered SOLELY on the basis of the information contained in the following passage.

Of those arrested in the city in 1983 for felonies or misdemeanors, only 32% were found guilty of any charge. Fifty-six percent of such arrestees were acquitted or had their cases dismissed, 11% failed to appear for trial, and 1% received other dispositions. Of those found guilty, only 7.4% received any sentences of over one year in jail. Only 50% of those found guilty were sentenced to any further time in jail. When considered with the low probability of arrests for most crimes, these figures make it clear that the crime control system in the city poses little threat to the average criminal. Delay compounds the problem. The average case took four appearances for disposition after arraignment. Twenty percent of all cases took eight or more appearances to reach a disposition. Forty-four percent of all cases took more than one year to disposition.

21. According to the above passage, crime statistics for 1983 indicate that   21.____

   A. there is a low probability of arrests for all crimes in the city
   B. the average criminal has much to fear from the law in the city
   C. over 10% of arrestees in the city charged with felonies or misdemeanors did not show up for trial
   D. criminals in the city are less likely to be caught than criminals in the rest of the country t

22. The percentage of those arrested in 1983 who received sentences of over one year in jail amounted MOST NEARLY to   22.____

   A. .237   B. 2.4   C. 23.7   D. 24.0

23. According to the above passage, the percentage of arrestees in 1983 who were found guilty was   23.____

   A. 20% of those arrested for misdemeanors
   B. 11% of those arrested for felonies
   C. 50% of those sentenced to further time in jail
   D. 32% of those arrested for felonies or misdemeanors

24. According to the above paragraph, the number of appearances after arraignment and before disposition amounted to

    24.____

    A. an average of four
    B. eight or more in 44% of the cases
    C. over four for cases which took more than a year
    D. between four and eight for most cases

Questions 25-27.

DIRECTIONS: Questions 25 through 27 are to be answered SOLELY on the basis of the information contained in the following paragraph.

    The traditional characteristics of a police organization, which do not foster group-centered leadership, are being changed daily by progressive police administrators. These characteristics are authoritarian and result in a leader-centered style with all determination of policy and procedure made by the leader. In the group-centered style, policies and procedures are a matter for group discussion and decision. The supposedly modern view is that the group-centered style is the most conducive to improving organizational effectiveness. By contrast, the traditional view regards the group-centered style as an idealistic notion of psychologists. It is questionable, however, that the situation determines the appropriate leadership style. In some circumstances, it will be leader-centered; in others, group-centered. Nevertheless, police supervisors will see more situations calling for a leadership style that, while flexible, is primarily group-centered. Thus, the supervisor in a police department must have a capacity not just to issue orders but to engage in behavior involving organizational leadership which primarily emphasizes goals and work facilitation.

25. According to the above passage, there is reason to believe that with regard to the effectiveness of different types of leadership, the

    25.____

    A. leader-centered type is better than the individual-centered type or the group-centered type
    B. leader-centered type is best in some situations and the group-centered type best in other situations
    C. group-centered type is better than the leader-centered type in all situations
    D. authoritarian type is least effective in democratic countries

26. According to the above passage, police administrators today are

    26.____

    A. more likely than in the past to favor making decisions on the basis of discussions with subordinates
    B. likely in general to favor traditional patterns of leadership in their organizations
    C. more likely to be progressive than conservative
    D. practical and individualistic rather than idealistic in their approach to police problems

27. According to the above passage, the role of the police department is changing in such a way that its supervisors must

    27.____

    A. give greater consideration to the needs of individual subordinates
    B. be more flexible in dealing with infractions of department rules

C. provide leadership which stresses the goals of the department and helps the staff to reach them
D. refrain from issuing orders and allow subordinates to decide how to carry out their assignments

Questions 28-31.

DIRECTIONS: Questions 28 through 31 are to be answered SOLELY on the basis of the information contained in the following paragraph.

Under the provisions of the Bank Protection Act of 1968, enacted July 8, 1968, each Federal banking supervisory agency, as of January 7, 1969, had to issue rules establishing minimum standards with which financial institutions under their control must comply with respect to the installation, maintenance, and operation of security devices and procedures, reasonable in cost, to discourage robberies, burglaries, and larcenies, and to assist in the identification and apprehension of persons who commit such acts. The rules set the time limits within which the affected banks and savings and loan associations must comply with the standards, and the rules require the submission of periodic reports on the steps taken. A violator of a rule under this Act is subject to a civil penalty not to exceed $100 for each day of the violation. The enforcement of these regulations rests with the responsible banking supervisory agencies.

28. The Bank Protection Act of 1968 was designed to

    A. provide Federal police protection for banks covered by the Act
    B. have organizations covered by the Act take precautions against criminals
    C. set up a system for reporting all bank robberies to the FBI
    D. insure institutions covered by the Act from financial loss due to robberies, burglaries, and larcenies

29. Under the provisions of the Bank Protection Act of 1968, each Federal banking supervisory agency was required to set up rules for financial institutions covered by the Act governing the

    A. hiring of personnel
    B. punishment of burglars
    C. taking of protective measures
    D. penalties for violations

30. Financial institutions covered by the Bank Protection Act of 1968 were required to

    A. file reports at regular intervals on what they had done to prevent theft
    B. identify and apprehend persons who commit robberies, burglaries, and larcenies
    C. draw up a code of ethics for their employees
    D. have fingerprints of their employees filed with the FBI

31. Under the provisions of the Bank Protection Act of 1968, a bank which is subject to the rules established under the Act and which violates a rule is liable to a penalty of NOT _____ than $100 for each _____.

    A. more; violation
    B. less; day of violation
    C. less; violation
    D. more; day of violation

Questions 32-36.

DIRECTIONS: Questions 32 through 36 are to be answered SOLELY on the basis of the information contained in the following paragraph.

A statement which is offered in an attempt to prove the truth of the matters therein stated, but which is not made by the author as a witness before the court at the particular trial in which it is so offered, is hearsay. This is so whether the statement consists of words (oral or written), of symbols used as a substitute for words, or of signs or other conduct offered as the equivalent of a statement. Subject to some well-established exceptions, hearsay is not generally acceptable as evidence, and it does not become competent evidence just because it is received by the court without objection. One basis for this rule is simply that a fact cannot be proved by showing that somebody stated it was a fact. Another basis for the rule is the fundamental principle that in a criminal prosecution the testimony of the witness shall be taken before the court, so that at the time he gives the testimony offered in evidence he will be sworn and subject to cross-examination, the scrutiny of the court, and confrontation by the accused.

32.   Which of the following is hearsay? A(n)   32.____

    A.   written statement by a person not present at the court hearing where the statement is submitted as proof of an occurrence
    B.   oral statement in court by a witness of what he saw
    C.   written statement of what he saw by a witness present in court
    D.   re-enactment by a witness in court of what he saw

33.   In a criminal case, a statement by a person not present in court is   33.____

    A.   *acceptable* evidence if not objected to by the prosecutor
    B.   *acceptable* evidence if not objected to by the defense lawyer
    C.   *not acceptable* evidence except in certain well-settled circumstances
    D.   *not acceptable* evidence under any circumstances

34.   The rule on hearsay is founded on the belief that   34.____

    A.   proving someone said an act occurred is not proof that the act did occur
    B.   a person who has knowledge about a case should be willing to appear in court
    C.   persons not present in court are likely to be unreliable witnesses
    D.   permitting persons to testify without appearing in court will lead to a disrespect for law

35.   One reason for the general rule that a witness in a criminal case must give his testimony   35.____
in court is that

    A.   a witness may be influenced by threats to make untrue statements
    B.   the opposite side is then permitted to question him
    C.   the court provides protection for a witness against unfair questioning
    D.   the adversary system is designed to prevent a miscarriage of justice

36.   Of the following, the MOST appropriate title for the above passage would be   36.____

    A.   WHAT IS HEARSAY?   B.   RIGHTS OF DEFENDANTS
    C.   TRIAL PROCEDURES   D.   TESTIMONY OF WITNESSES

Questions 37-40.

DIRECTIONS: Questions 37 through 40 are to be answered SOLELY on the basis *of* the following graphs.

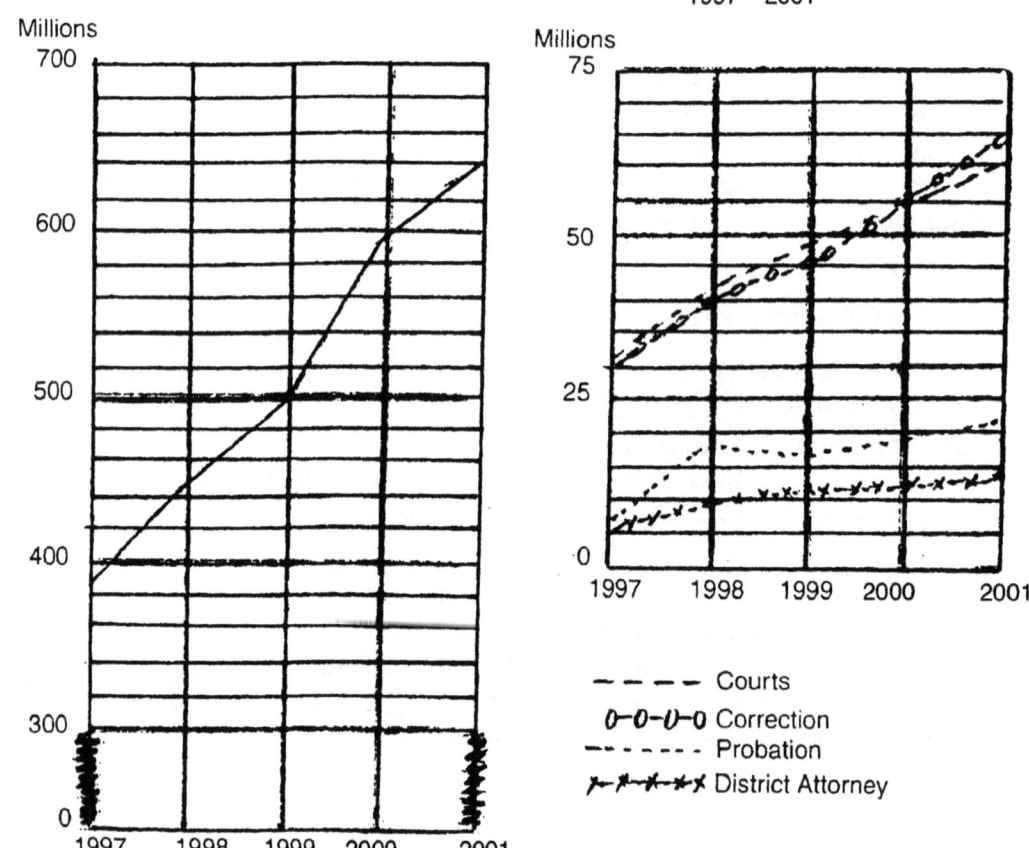

37. In 2001, the amount of money budgeted for courts amounted to APPROXIMATELY what   37.____
    percentage of the amount of money budgeted for police?

    A. 10%   B. 20%   C. 30%   D. 40%

38. In 2000, the police budget exceeded the sum of amounts budgeted for the four other   38.____
    criminal justice expenditures MOST NEARLY by

    A. $410,000,000   B. $459,000,000
    C. $475,000,000   D. $487,000,000

39. Between which of the following years did the amount of money budgeted for one cate-   39.____
    gory of criminal justice decrease by about one million dollars?

    A. 1997-1998   B. 1998-1999
    C. 1999-2000   D. 2000-2001

40. If the 1998 dollar was worth 96% of the 1997 dollar and the 1999 dollar was worth 90% of the 1997 dollar, the increase in the budget for Correction from 1998 to 1999, in terms of the 1997 dollar, amounted to 40.____

   A. $2,100,000
   C. $4,320,000
   B. $4,200,000
   D. $4,700,000

KEY (CORRECT ANSWERS)

1. A	11. C	21. C	31. D
2. B	12. B	22. B	32. A
3. B	13. D	23. D	33. C
4. C	14. C	24. A	34. A
5. D	15. D	25. B	35. B
6. C	16. D	26. A	36. A
7. D	17. C	27. C	37. A
8. B	18. C	28. B	38. B
9. C	19. D	29. C	39. B
10. A	20. D	30. A	40. A

EXAMINATION SECTION
TEST 1

DIRECTIONS: Each question or incomplete statement is followed by several suggested answers or completions. Select the one that BEST answers the question or completes the statement. *PRINT THE LETTER OF THE CORRECT ANSWER IN THE SPACE AT THE RIGHT.*

1. The process of determining the quantity of goods and materials that are in stock is commonly called   1._____

    A. receiving   B. disbursement
    C. reconciliation   D. inventory

2. Proper and effective storage procedure involves the storing of   2._____

    A. items together on the basis of class grouping
    B. all items in chronological order based on date received
    C. items in alphabetical order based on date of delivery
    D. items randomly wherever space is available

3. Which of the following is the FIRST step involved in correctly taking an inventory?   3._____

    A. Reconciliation of inventory records with the number of items on hand
    B. Analysis of possible discrepancies between items on hand and the stock record balance
    C. Identification and recording of the locations of all items in stock
    D. Issuance of an inventory directive to all vendors

4. Supply items other than food which are subject to deterioration should be checked   4._____

    A. at delivery time only   B. occasionally
    C. only when issued   D. periodically

5. For which of the following supplies is it MOST necessary to provide ample ventilation?   5._____

    A. Small rubber parts   B. Metal products
    C. Flammable liquids   D. Wooden items

6. Storing small lots of supplies in an area designated for the storage of large lots of supplies will generally result in   6._____

    A. *loss* of supplies   B. *loss* of storage space
    C. *increase* in inventory   D. *increase* in storage space

7. Compliance with fire preventive measures is a major requirement for the maintenance of a safe warehouse. Which of the following statements is LEAST important in describing a measure useful in maintaining a fire preventive facility?   7._____

    A. Smoking is only permitted in designated areas.
    B. Oil-soaked rags should be disposed of promptly and not stored.
    C. When not in use, electrical machinery should be grounded.
    D. Gasoline-powered materials handling equipment should not be refueled with the motor running.

8. It is POOR storage practice to store small valuable items loosely in open containers in bulk storage areas because doing so results in the

    A. misplacement of such items
    B. pilferage of these items
    C. deterioration of such supplies
    D. hindrance in inspection of these supplies

8.____

9. Assume that you have been placed in charge of the receiving operations at your garage. Generally, you receive all the supplies you order during the first week of each month. Of the following, the MOST effective and economic way to facilitate receiving operations would be to

    A. secure overtime authorization for laborers during that week
    B. have all truck deliveries made in one day
    C. stagger truck deliveries throughout each morning of the week
    D. assign all personnel to receiving duty for that week

9.____

10. Effective security measures must be instituted to provide for the safekeeping of city supplies.
However, the scope and complexity of security measures used at a warehouse facility should correspond MOST NEARLY to the

    A. value of supplies stored in the warehouse
    B. borough in which the warehouse is located
    C. level of warehouse activity
    D. age of the warehouse facility

10.____

11. To facilitate handling and issuance of supply items that have a high turnover rate, they should generally be stored

    A. away from accessible aisles
    B. on upper shelves
    C. in a locked compartment area
    D. close to the service counter area

11.____

12. The MOST important factor to be considered in effectively storing heavy, bulky, and difficult-to-handle items is to store these items

    A. as close to shipping areas as possible
    B. in storage areas with a low floor-load capacity
    C. only in outside storage sheds
    D. away from aisles

12.____

Questions 13-16.

DIRECTIONS: Questions 13 through 16 are to be answered using ONLY the information in the following passage.

Fire exit drills should be established and held periodically to effectively train personnel to leave their working area promptly upon proper signal and to evacuate the building speedily but without confusion. All fire exit drills should be carefully planned and carried out in a serious manner under rigid discipline so as to provide positive protection in the event of a real emergency. As a general rule, the local fire department should be furnished advance information regarding the exact date and time the exit drill is scheduled. When it is impossible to hold regular drills, written instructions should be distributed to all employees.

Depending upon individual circumstances, fires in warehouses vary from those of fast development that are almost instantly beyond any possibility of employee control to others of relatively slow development where a small readily attackable flame may be present for periods of time up to 15 minutes or more during which simple attack with fire extinguishers or small building hoses may prevent the fire development. In any case, it is characteristic of many warehouse fires that at a certain point in development they flash up to the top of the stack, increase heat quickly, and spread rapidly. There is a degree of inherent danger in attacking warehouse type fires and all employees should be thoroughly trained in the use of the types of extinguishers or small hoses in the buildings and well instructed in the necessity of always staying between the fire and a direct pass to an exit.

13. Employees should be instructed that, when fighting a fire, they MUST   13._____

    A. try to control the blaze
    B. extinguish any fire in 15 minutes
    C. remain between the fire and a direct passage to the exit
    D. keep the fire between themselves and the fire exit

14. Whenever conditions are such that regular fire drills cannot be held, then which one of   14._____
the following actions should be taken?

    A. The local fire department should be notified.
    B. Rigid discipline should be maintained during work hours.
    C. Personnel should be instructed to leave their working area by whatever means are available.
    D. Employees should receive fire drill procedures in writing.

15. The passage indicates that the purpose of fire exit drills is to train employees to   15._____

    A. control a fire before it becomes uncontrollable
    B. act as firefighters
    C. leave the working area promptly
    D. be serious

16. According to the passage, fire exit drills will prove to be of *utmost* effectiveness if   16._____

    A. employee participation is made voluntary
    B. they take place periodically
    C. the fire department actively participates
    D. they are held without advance planning

Questions 17-20.

DIRECTIONS: Questions 17 through 20 are to be answered using ONLY the information in the following paragraph.

A report is frequently ineffective because the person writing it is not fully acquainted with all the necessary details before he actually starts to construct the report. All details pertaining to the subject should be known before the report is started. If the essential facts are not known, they should be investigated. It is wise to have essential facts written down rather than to depend too much on memory, especially if the facts pertain to such matters as amounts, dates, names of persons, or other specific data. When the necessary information has been gathered, the general plan and content of the report should be thought out before the writing is actually begun. A person with little or no experience in writing reports may find that it is wise to make a brief outline. Persons with more experience should not need a written outline, but they should make mental notes of the steps they are to follow. If writing reports without dictation is a regular part of an office worker's duties, he should set aside a certain time during the day when he is least likely to be interrupted. That may be difficult, but in most offices there are certain times in the day when the callers, telephone calls, and other interruptions are not numerous. During those times, it is best to write reports that need undivided concentration. Reports that are written amid a series of interruptions may be poorly done.

17. Before starting to write an effective report, it is necessary to   17.____

     A. memorize all specific information
     B. disregard ambiguous data
     C. know all pertinent information
     D. develop a general plan

18. Reports dealing with complex and difficult material should be   18.____

     A. prepared and written by the supervisor of the unit
     B. written when there is the least chance of interruption
     C. prepared and written as part of regular office routine
     D. outlined and then dictated

19. According to the passage, employees with no prior familiarity in writing reports may find it helpful to   19.____

     A. prepare a brief outline
     B. mentally prepare a synopsis of the report's content
     C. have a fellow employee help in writing the report
     D. consult previous reports

20. In writing a report, needed information which is unclear should be   20.____

     A. disregarded   B. investigated
     C. memorized   D. gathered

———————

KEY (CORRECT ANSWERS)

1.	D	11.	D
2.	A	12.	A
3.	C	13.	C
4.	D	14.	D
5.	C	15.	C
6.	B	16.	B
7.	C	17.	C
8.	B	18.	B
9.	C	19.	A
10.	A	20.	B

___

TEST 2

DIRECTIONS: Each question or incomplete statement is followed by several suggested answers or completions. Select the one that BEST answers the question or completes the statement. *PRINT THE LETTER OF THE CORRECT ANSWER IN THE SPACE AT THE RIGHT.*

Questions 1-4.

DIRECTIONS: Questions 1 through 4 are to be answered using ONLY the information in the following passage.

The operation and maintenance of the stock-location system is a warehousing function and responsibility. The stock locator system shall consist of a file of stock-location record cards, either manually or mechanically prepared, depending upon the equipment available. The file shall contain an individual card for each stock item stored in the depot, with the records maintained in stock number sequence.

The locator file is used for all receiving, warehousing, inventory, and shipping activities in the depot. The locator file must contain complete and accurate data to provide ready support to the various depot functions and activities, i.e., processing shipping documents, updating records on mechanized equipment, where applicable, supplying accurate locator information for stock selection and proper storage of receipts, consolidating storage locations of identical items not subject to shelf-life control, and preventing the consolidation of stock of limited shelf-life items. The file is also essential in accomplishing location surveys and the inventory program.

Storage of bulk stock items by "spot-location" method is generally recognized as the best means of obtaining maximum warehouse space utilization. Despite the fact that the spot-location method of storage enables full utilization of storage capacity, this method may prove inefficient unless it is supplemented by adequate stock-location control, including proper lay-out and accurate maintenance of stock locator cards.

1. The manner in which the stock-location record cards should be filed is   1.____

    A. alphabetically   B. chronologically
    C. numerically   D. randomly

2. Items of limited shelf-life should   2.____

    A. not be stored
    B. not be stored together
    C. be stored in stock sequence
    D. be stored together

3. Which one of the following is NOT mentioned in the passage as a use of the stock-location system?   3.____
Aids in

    A. accomplishing location surveys
    B. providing information for stock selection
    C. storing items received for the first time
    D. processing shipping documents

4. If the spot-location method of storing is used, then the use of the stock-location system is   4._____

    A. *desirable,* because the stock-location system is recognized as the best means of obtaining maximum warehouse space utilization
    B. *undesirable,* because additional records must be kept
    C. *desirable,* because stock-location controls are necessary with the spot-location storage method
    D. *undesirable,* because a stock-locator system will take up valuable storage space

Questions 5-8.

DIRECTIONS: Questions 5 through 8 are to be answered using ONLY the information in the following paragraph.

    Known damage is defined as damage that is apparent and acknowledged by the carrier at the time of delivery to the purchaser. A meticulous inspection of the damaged goods should be completed by the purchaser and a notation specifying the extent of the damage should be applied to the carrier's original freight bill. As is the case in known loss, it is necessary for the carrier's agent to acknowledge by signature the damage notation in order for it to have any legal status. The purchaser should not refuse damaged freight since it is his legal duty to accept the property and to employ every available and reasonable means to protect the shipment and minimize the loss. Acceptance of a damaged shipment does not endanger any legitimate claim the purchaser may have against the carrier for damage. If the purchaser fails to observe the legal duty to accept damaged freight, the carrier may consider it abandoned. After properly notifying the vendor and purchaser of his intentions, the carrier may dispose of the material at public sale.

5. Before disposing of an abandoned shipment, the carrier must   5._____

    A. notify the vendor and the carrier's agent
    B. advise the vendor and purchaser of his plans
    C. notify the purchaser and the carrier's agent
    D. obtain the signature of the carrier's agent on the freight bill

6. In the case of damaged freight, the original freight bill will only have legal value if it is signed by the   6._____

    A. carrier's agent   B. purchaser
    C. vendor   D. purchaser and vendor

7. A purchaser does not protect a shipment of cargo that is damaged and is further deteriorating.   7._____
According to the above paragraph, the action of the purchaser is

    A. *acceptable,* because he is not obligated to protect damaged cargo
    B. *unacceptable,* because damaged cargo must be protected no matter what is involved
    C. *acceptable,* because he took possession of the cargo
    D. *unacceptable,* because he is obligated by law to protect the cargo

8. The TWO requirements that must be satisfied before cargo can be labeled *known dam-*   8.____
    age are signs of evident damage and

    A. confirmation by the carrier or carrier's agent that this is so
    B. delayed shipment of goods
    C. signature of acceptance by the purchaser
    D. acknowledgment by the vendor that this is so

Questions 9-13.

DIRECTIONS: Questions 9 through 13 are to be answered on the basis of the following graph.

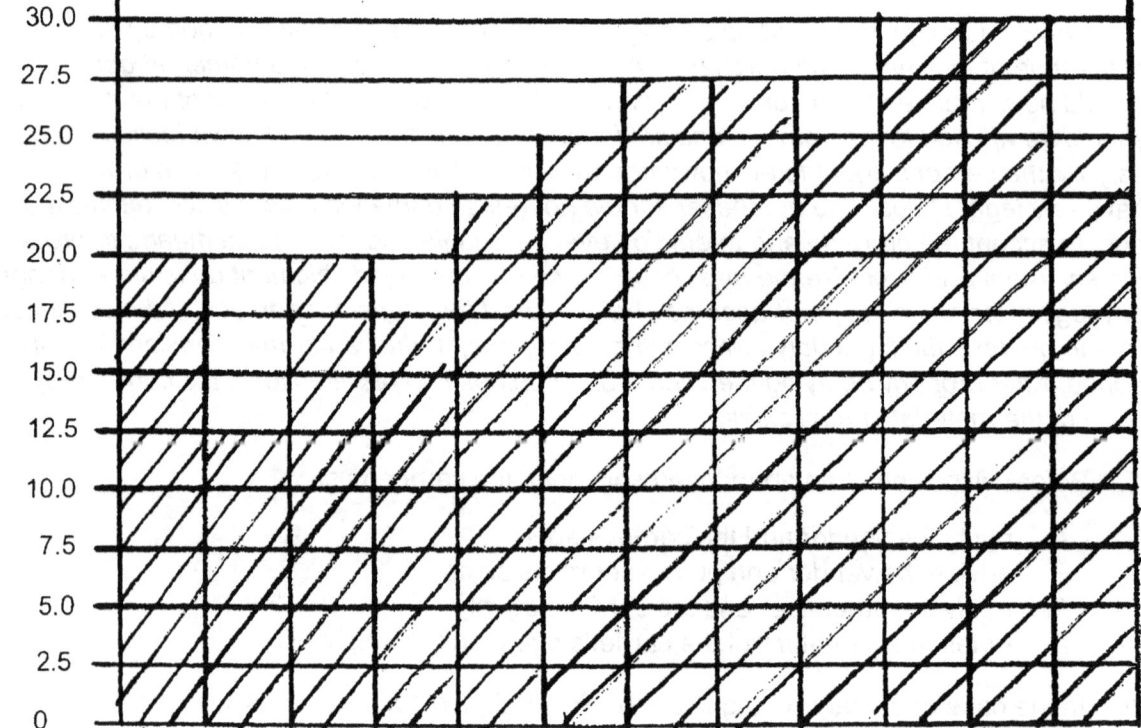

GARBAGE COLLECTIONS MADE JAN. 1 - DEC. 31, IN TONS (SHORT TON)

9. According to the information presented in the graph, the weight of the average monthly   9.____
    collection of garbage is
    MOST NEARLY _____ tons.

    A. 22.5   B. 23.5   C. 24.5   D. 25.5

10. If a truck can carry 6,000 lbs., then the number of truck-loads collected during the year   10.____
    was MOST NEARLY

    A. 55   B. 75   C. 95   D. 115

11. The amount of garbage collected during the second half of the year represents   11.____
    APPROXIMATELY what percentage of the total garbage collected during the year?

    A. 50%   B. 60%   C. 70%   D. 80%

12. During the months of September, October, and November, approximately 12% of the col- 12.____
    lections consisted of fallen leaves.
    What was the weight of the remaining garbage NOT containing fallen leaves for that
    period?
    _____ tons.

    A. 10   B. 20   C. 65   D. 75

13. Assume that the collections for the year as shown in the above graph exceeded the pre- 13.____
    vious year's collection by 17%. The collection made in the previous year was MOST
    NEARLY _____ tons.

    A. 50   B. 225   C. 240   D. 275   .

Questions 14-17.

DIRECTIONS: Questions 14 through 17 are to be answered on the basis of the following
              graph

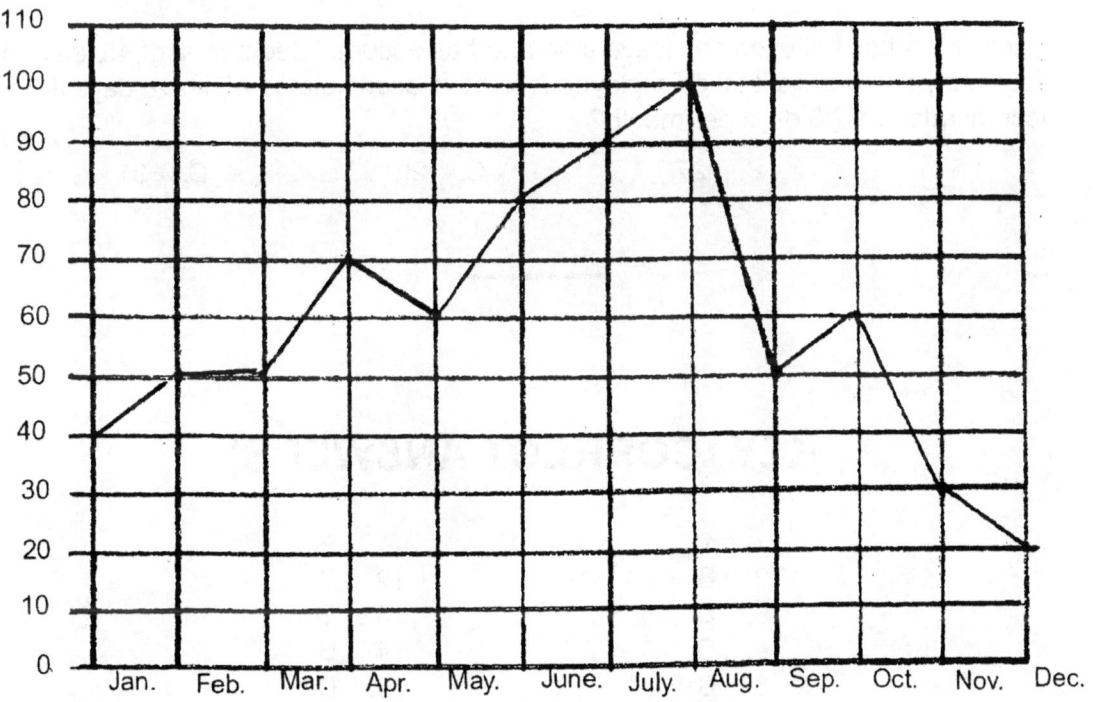

INVENTORY LEVELS (IN DOZENS) OF ITEM A IN STOREHOUSE
AT BEGINNING OF MONTH FOR A PERIOD OF TWELVS MONTH

14. The average monthly inventory level during the course of the year was MOST NEARLY 14.____
    _____ dozen.

    A. 45   B. 60   C. 75   D. 90

15. If one dozen items fit in a carton measuring 2 feet by 2 feet by 3 feet, what MINIMUM vol- 15.____
    ume would be required to store the maximum August inventory?
    _____ cubic feet.

    A. 12   B. 100   C. 700   D. 1,200

29

16. Assume that deliveries are made to the storehouse on the first working day of each month. If 30% of the June inventory was consumed during the month, how many items had to be delivered to reach the July inventory level?
_____ items.

    A. 288   B. 408   C. 696   D. 1,080

16.____

17. Which three-month period contained the LOWEST average inventory level?

    A. Jan., Feb., March   B. April, May, June
    C. July, Aug., Sept.   D. Oct., Nov., Dec.

17.____

18. Assume that it takes approximately 1 1/2 minutes to unload a dozen identical items from a delivery truck.
At this speed, the amount of time it should take to unload a shipment of 876 items is MOST NEARLY _____ minutes.

    A. 90   B. 100   C. 110   D. 120

18.____

19. Assume that a shop clerk has received a bill of $108 for a delivery of clamps which cost $4.32 per dozen.
How many clamps should there be in this delivery?

    A. 25   B. 36   C. 300   D. 360

19.____

20. Employee A has not used any leave time and has accumulated a total of 45 leave days. How many months did it take Employee A to have accumulated 45 leave days if the accrual rate is 1 2/3 days per month?

    A. 25   B. 27   C. 29   D. 31

20.____

KEY (CORRECT ANSWERS)

1.	C	11.	B
2.	B	12.	D
3.	C	13.	C
4.	C	14.	B
5.	B	15.	D
6.	A	16.	B
7.	D	17.	D
8.	A	18.	C
9.	B	19.	C
10.	C	20.	B

EXAMINATION SECTION
TEST 1

DIRECTIONS: Each question or incomplete statement is followed by several suggested answers or completions. Select the one that BEST answers the question or completes the statement. *PRINT THE LETTER OF THE CORRECT ANSWER IN THE SPACE AT THE RIGHT.*

Questions 1-4.

DIRECTIONS: Questions 1 through 4 are to be answered using only the information in the following passage.

Planning for storage layout in terms of the supplies to be stored involves the intelligent and realistic application of a stockman's basic resources - space. The main objective of storage planning is the maximum use of available space. The planning and layout of space are dependent upon the types of supplies expected to be stored, and certain characteristics must be considered. Some supplies must be protected from dampness, extreme changes of temperature, and other such conditions. Iron and steel products rust quickly at high temperatures with high humidity. High temperatures also cause some plastics to melt and change shape, while extreme dampness can cause paper to mildew and wood to warp. Hazardous articles, including flammable items like paint and rubber cement, should be stored separated from each other and from other types of supplies.

Extremes in characteristics such as size, shape, and weight need to be considered in laying out space. Large, awkward containers and unusually heavy items generally should be stored near doors with aisles leading directly to them and/or shipping and receiving facilities. Light and fragile items cannot be stacked to a height which would cause crushing or other damage to containers and contents. Fast-moving articles should be stored in locations from which they can be handled quickly and efficiently.

1. It is MOST important to store articles like paints and rubber cement in areas where   1._____

   A. they can be protected from theft
   B. shipping and receiving doors are easily accessible
   C. they can be isolated from other supplies
   D. boxes containing them can be stacked as high as possible

2. Storage locations from which items can be selected and issued quickly are recommended for supplies classified as   2._____

   A. fragile   B. fast-moving
   C. under-sized   D. flammable

3. In order to prevent supplies made of iron from rusting, they should be stored in areas with _____ humidity and _____ temperature.   3._____

   A. low; high   B. low; low
   C. high; high   D. high; low

4. Which of the following characteristics is NOT considered in the above passage on storage planning and layout?
The _____ of the item to be stored.   4._____

   A. size   B. quantity   C. weight   D. shape

Questions 5-12.

DIRECTIONS: Each of Questions 5 through 12 consists of a word in capitals followed by four suggested meanings of the word. For each question, choose the meaning which you think is BEST and print the letter of the correct answer in the space at the right.

5. CATALOG   5.____

    A. to list   B. to rate   C. to print   D. to price

6. DURABLE   6.____

    A. smooth   B. sticky   C. lasting   D. feeling

7. MUTUAL   7.____

    A. silent   B. shared   C. changing   D. broken

8. REJECT   8.____

    A. rewrite   B. refuse   C. release   D. regret

9. OBSTRUCT   9.____

    A. teach   B. darken   C. block   D. resist

10. CORRODE   10.____

    A. melt   B. rust   C. burn   D. warp

11. EXCESS   11.____

    A. surplus   B. storage   C. spacing   D. survey

12. FLEXIBLE   12.____

    A. neatly folded   B. easily broken
    C. easily bent   D. neatly piled

Questions 13-16.

DIRECTIONS: Questions 13 through 16 are to be answered using ONLY the information in the following passage.

The "active stock" portion of the inventory is that portion which is kept for the purpose of satisfying the shop's expected requirements of that material. It is directly related to the "order quantity." The "order quantity" is found by determining the expected annual requirements of the shop and dividing this by the number of orders for this merchandise which will be placed during the year. The most economical number of orders is usually found by considering the cost of ordering and storing inventory.

The "safety stock" portion of the inventory is that portion which is created to take care of above-average or unexpected demands on the inventory. This portion is directly related to the point at which the order is placed. The amount of safety stock is not determined by com-

paring order costs and carrying costs, but on the need for protection against stock shortages for each stock item under consideration. Some stock items will need more safety stock than others, depending upon how much difference there has been in the past between the expected usage of material and the actual amount needed and used for any given time period, plus the reliability of the suppliers' delivery and of the order lead-time. If the expected usage of an item has always been 100% accurately predicted, then theoretically there would be no need for "safety stock."

13. According to the above passage, the *active stock* inventory is that portion of the inventory which is   13._____

    A. used most frequently by management
    B. ordered on a regular basis, such as every month
    C. expected to meet the organization's anticipated inventory needs
    D. needed to protect against shortages in very active inventory items

14. According to the above passage, what factors must be considered to determine the order quantity for any active stock item?   14._____

    A. Anticipated requirements, ordering cost, and cost of storing inventory
    B. Order lead-time and delivery service
    C. Variety of stock items ordered in the previous year
    D. The largest quantity ever ordered

15. Maintaining a safety stock portion of the inventory is   15._____

    A. *good,* because it provides for unexpected demands on the inventory
    B. *good,* because it makes the inventory more valuable than it actually is
    C. *poor,* because it provides unnecessary work for stockmen since the Inventory is rarely used
    D. *poor,* because it makes storage areas overcrowded and unsafe

16. The above passage indicates that 100 percent accuracy in forecasting future activity will eliminate the need for   16._____

    A. reliable deliveries
    B. active stock
    C. safety stock
    D. deviation in total order quantity

17. At the start of a certain month, you have 185 jars of glue in stock. During that month, you fill the following orders: 3 orders for 12 jars each, 2 orders for 10 jars each, 2 orders for 8 jars each, one order for 9 jars, one order for 20 jars, and one order for 24 jars.
If you received no shipments of glue during that month, the number of jars of glue you will have on hand at the end of the month is   17._____

    A. 60   B. 77   C. 102   D. 125

18. Assume that you are ordering merchandise from a vendor who gives a discount of 10%, plus an additional 2% for payment within 30 days.
If, on October 21st, you order merchandise which has a catalogue value of $714, and the bill is paid by November 10th, the net amount of the payment should be MOST NEARLY   18._____

    A. $628.32   B. $629.95   C. $630.74   D. $632.60

19. Suppose that there are 293 people in your shop and 11% of them are women.   19.___
    The number of men in your shop is

    A.   261   B.   263   C.   269   D.   271

20. In March, Department Z made an overpayment of $34.26 to the Superior Fuel Oil Com-   20.___
    pany. This amount was credited to the Department's account. In April, the fuel bill
    amounted to $378.12.
    Considering the credit on the Department's account, the payment that should be remit-
    ted for the April fuel bill is

    A. $343.86   B. $343.96   C. $344.86   D. $344.96

21. A certain agency ordered and used 1,020 one-pound balls of twine last year at a total   21.___
    cost of $357.
    If the price per ball of twine remained constant throughout the year, the cost of each
    one-pound ball was

    A.   25¢   B.   30¢   C.   35¢   D.   40¢

22. You place an order at the Abbey Office Supply Company for three of each of the following   22.___
    items: metal desk at $129 each; chair at $65 each; desk lamp at $24 each.
    If this supply company gives a 15% discount on all orders totaling $500 or more, the
    net price of this order is

    A. $567.90   B. $555.90   C. $484.20   D. $479.20

23. Suppose that there are 27 people in your department and your boss tells you that he is   23.___
    putting on an extra laborer and two mechanics.
    The percent of the Increase in personnel for your department would be MOST
    NEARLY

    A.   8%   B.   9%   C.   10%   D.   11%

Questions 24-29.

DIRECTIONS:

CODE TABLE

Code Letter	b	d	f	a	g	s	z	w	h	u
Code Number	1	2	3	4	5	6	7	8	9	0

In the Code Table above, each code letter has a corresponding code number directly
beneath it.

Each of Questions 24 through 29 contains three sets of code letters and code numbers.
In each set, the code numbers should correspond with the code letters as given in the table,
but there is a coding error in some of the sets. Examine the sets in each question carefully.

Mark your answer:
    A if there is a coding error in only ONE of the sets in the question;
    B if there is a coding error in any TWO of the sets in the question;
    C if there is a coding error in all THREE sets in the question;
    D if there is a coding error in NONE of the sets in the question.

SAMPLE QUESTION:

    fgzduwaf - 35720843
    uabsdgfw - 04262538
    hhfaudgs - 99340257

In the sample question above, the first set is right because each code number matches the code letter as in the Code Table. In the second set, the corresponding number for the code letter b is wrong because it should be 1 instead of 2. In the third set, the corresponding number for the last code letter s is wrong because it should be 6 instead of 7. Since there is an error in two of the sets, the answer to the above sample question is B.

24.   fsbughwz - 36104987   24.____
       zwubgasz - 78025467
       ghgufddb - 59583221

25.   hafgdaas - 94351446   25.____
       ddsfabsd - 22734162
       wgdbssgf - 85216553

26.   abfbssbd - 41316712   26.____
       ghzfaubs - 59734017
       sdbzfwza - 62173874

27.   whfbdzag - 89412745   27.____
       daaszuub - 24467001
       uzhfwssd - 07936623

28.   zbadgbuh - 71425109   28.____
       dzadbbsz - 27421167
       gazhwaff - 54798433

29.   fbfuadsh - 31304265   29.____
       gzfuwzsb - 57300671
       bashhgag - 14699535

Questions 30-35.

DIRECTIONS: Questions 30 through 35 are to be answered on the basis of the information in the Weekly Requisition Form below.

WEEKLY REQUISITION FORM

Storehouse 17	Date 7.17	Dept. Code 809	Dept. Budget Code 13942	Dept. Requisition No. 1029		
Deliver to: Requisition Dept. Atlantic Hospital			Unit and/or Division Kitchen	Address 66 W. Highland Blvd.		
Storehouse Item Code	Description Incl. Size, Number or Measurements		Unit of Issue	No. Units Requested	Unit Price	Tot. Cost
895	Chocolate Syrup #10 can		case	5	7.35	
1926	Mayonnaise 1 gal. jar		case	2	6.73	13.46
1945	B1ack pepper, ground 1.lb. can		lb	3		1.89
1976	34 fresh eggs			7	.41	2.87
220	Pineapple, crushed #10 can		case	4	5.89	23.56
5395	Straws 8 1/2" long 500 to box		box	12	.47	5.64
452	Applesauce 4 1/2 oz. jar 24/case		case		1.65	6.60
Requested By John Smith	Title Shop Clerk	Material Issued By _____ Date _____		Material Received By Signed _____ Date _____		
_____ Approved By	Supervisor	Total No. Pieces _____		Total No. Pieces _____		

30. What is the total cost of the chocolate syrup order described in the requisition form above?   30. ____

   A. $36.75   B. $34.35   C. $31.65   D. $30.15

31. The week of 7/24, the price of a gallon jar of mayonnaise increased by 4 cents. If there are 6 gallon jars of mayonnaise per case, how much is the total cost of the mayonnaise order for the week of 7/24, if the order quantity is the same as the previous week?   31. ____

   A. $6.97   B. $7.21   C. $13.68   D. $13.94

32. What is the unit price for ground black pepper as described in the requisition form above?   32. ____

   A. 36¢   B. 43¢   C. 57¢   D. 63¢

33. Based on the information provided in the requisition form above, what is the correct unit of issue for fresh eggs?   33. ____

   A. Each   B. Container   C. Dozen   D. Case

34. There are 6 #10 cans of crushed pineapple per case. Based on the information in the requisition form above, how many #10 cans of pineapple are being ordered?   34. ____

   A. 16   B. 20   C. 24   D. 30

35. Each week the cook at Atlantic Hospital uses 84 4 1/2 ounce jars of applesauce. Based on the requisition for the week of 7/17, how many cases must be ordered to fill the need for the following week (7/24) in order to avoid storing an excess supply of applesauce? (Assume that there was no excess from the week previous to 7/17.)

    A. 1   B. 2   C. 3   D. 4

35.____

36. Suppose that the shop in which you worked received 421 pieces of mail in one month, of which 64 were requests for information.
The percent of letters which were requests for information is MOST NEARLY

    A. 13.2%   B. 15.2%   C. 15.5%   D. 16.1%

36.____

37. The following is the year's stock issue record of cans of oil distributed for use in Agency Y: January - 107; February - 94; March - 113; April - 118; May - 122; June - 87; July - 89; August - 98; September - 110; October - 101; November - 105; December - 106.
The monthly average of cans of oil distributed is MOST NEARLY

    A. 100   B. 102   C. 104   D. 106

37.____

38. Two trucks, A and B, are carrying stock from a warehouse to the shop. The weight of the truck alone is the tare; the weight of the loaded truck is the gross weight. Truck A has a tare of 4,637 pounds, and a gross weight of 6,955 pounds. Truck B has a tare of 4,489 pounds, and a gross weight of 6,723 pounds.
What is the total weight of the loads of both trucks?
_____ pounds.

    A. 3,452   B. 3,564   C. 4,552   D. 4,653

38.____

39. A stock carton measures 24" long, 18" wide, and 24" high. What is the maximum number of boxes measuring 4 1/2" long, 3" wide, and 3" high that can be packed inside the carton?

    A. 135   B. 256   C. 405   D. 432

39.____

40. If a ream of paper weighs 11 ounces, 36 reams of paper will weigh_____ pounds, _____ ounces.

    A. 22; 8   B. 24; 12   C. 33; 0   D. 39; 6

40.____

KEY (CORRECT ANSWERS)

1.	C	11.	A	21.	C	31.	D
2.	B	12.	C	22.	B	32.	D
3.	B	13.	C	23.	D	33.	C
4.	B	14.	A	24.	C	34.	C
5.	A	15.	A	25.	C	35.	C
6.	C	16.	C	26.	B	36.	B
7.	B	17.	A	27.	B	37.	C
8.	B	18.	A	28.	D	38.	C
9.	C	19.	A	29.	C	39.	B
10.	B	20.	A	30.	A	40.	B

———

TEST 2

DIRECTIONS: Each question or incomplete statement is followed by several suggested answers or completions. Select the one that BEST answers the question or completes the statement. *PRINT THE LETTER OF THE CORRECT ANSWER IN THE SPACE AT THE RIGHT.*

Questions 1-6.

DIRECTIONS: Questions 1 through 6 are to be answered on the basis of the information below.

A certain shop keeps an informational card file for all suppliers and merchandise. On each card is the supplier's name, the contract number for the merchandise he supplies, and a delivery date for the merchandise. In this filing system, the supplier's name is filed alphabetically, the contract number for the merchandise is filed numerically, and the delivery date is filed chronologically.

In Questions 1 through 6, there are five notations numbered 1 through 5 shown in Column I. Each notation is made up of a supplier's name, a contract number, and a date and is to be filed according to the following rules:

First: File in alphabetical order
Second: When two or more notations have the same supplier, file according to the contract number in numerical order beginning with the lowest number
Third: When two or more notations have the same supplier and contract number, file according to the date beginning with the earliest date

In Column II, the numbers 1 through 5 are arranged in four ways to show different possible orders in which the merchandise information might be filed. Pick the answer (A, B, C, or D) in Column II in which the notations are arranged according to the above filing rules.

SAMPLE QUESTION:

Column I
1. Cluney (4865) 6/17/72
2. Roster (2466) 5/10/71
3. Altool (7114) 10/15/72
4. Cluney (5276) 12/18/71
5. Cluney (4865) 4/8/72

Column II
A. 2, 3, 4, 1, 5
B. 2, 5, 1, 3, 4
C. 3, 2, 1, 4, 5
D. 3, 5, 1, 4, 2

The correct way to file the notations is:
(3) Altool (7114) 10/15/72
(5) Cluney (4865) 4/8/72
(1) Cluney (4865) 6/17/72
(4) Cluney (5276) 12/18/71
(2) Roster (2466) 5/10/71

Since the correct filing order is 3, 5, 1, 4, 2, the answer to the sample question is D.

Column I	Column II	
1.	1. Fenten (38511) 1/4/73 2. Meadowlane (5020) 11/1/72 3. Whitehall (36142) 6/22/72 4. Clinton (4141) 5/26/71 5. Mester (8006) 4/20/71	A. 3, 5, 2, 1, 4 B. 4, 1, 2, 5, 3 C. 4, 2, 5, 3, 1 D. 5, 4, 3, 1, 2	1.___
2.	1. Harvard (2286) 2/19/70 2. Parker (1781) 4/12/72 3. Lenson (9044) 6/6/72 4. Brothers (38380) 10/11/72 5. Parker (41400) 12/20/70	A. 2, 4, 3, 1, 5 B. 2, 1, 3, 4, 5 C. 4, 1, 3, 2, 5 D. 5, 2, 3, 1, 4	2.___
3.	1. Newtone (3197) 8/22/70 2. Merritt (4071) 8/8/72 3. Writebest (60666) 4/7/71 4. Maltons (34380) 3/30/72 5. Merrit (4071) 7/16/71	A. 1, 4, 2, 5, 3 B. 4, 2, 1, 5, 3 C. 4, 5, 2, 1, 3 D. 5, 2, 4, 3, 1	3.___
4.	1. Weinburt (45514) 6/4/71 2. Owntye (35860) 10/4/72 3. Weinburt (45515) 2/1/72 4. Fasttex (7677) 11/10/71 5. Owntye (4574) 7/17/72	A. 4, 5, 2, 1, 3 B. 4, 2, 5, 3, 1 C. 4, 2, 5, 1, 3 D. 4, 5, 2, 3, 1	4.___
5.	1. Premier (1003) 7/29/70 2. Phylson (0031) 5/5/72 3. Lathen (3328) 10/3/71 4. Harper (8046) 8/18/72 5. Lathen (3328) 12/1/72	A. 2, 1, 4, 3, 5 B. 3, 5, 4, 1, 2 C. 4, 1, 2, 3, 5 D. 4, 3, 5, 2, 1	5.___
6.	1. Repper (46071) 10/14/72 2. Destex (77271) 8/27/72 3. Clawson (30736) 7/28/71 4. Destex (27207) 8/17/71 5. Destex (77271) 4/14/71	A. 3, 2, 4, 5, 1 B. 3, 4, 2, 5, 1 C. 3, 4, 5, 2, 1 D. 3, 5, 4, 2, 1	6.___

7. Assume that a clerk is asked to prepare a special report which he has not prepared before. He decides to make a written outline of the report before writing it in full. This decision by the clerk is

   7.___

  A. *good,* mainly because it helps the writer to organize his thoughts and decide what will go into the report
  B. *good,* mainly because it clearly shows the number of topics, number of pages, and the length of the report
  C. *poor,* mainly because it wastes the time of the writer since he will have to write the full report anyway
  D. *poor,* mainly because it confines the writer to those areas listed in the outline

8. Assume that a clerk in the water resources central shop is asked to prepare an important report, giving the location and condition of various fire hydrants in the city. One of the hydrants in question is broken and is spewing rusty water in the street, creating a flooded condition in the area. The clerk reports that the hydrant is broken but does not report the escaping water or the flood.
Of the following, the BEST evaluation of the clerk's decision about what to report is that it is basically

8.____

   A. *correct,* chiefly because a lengthy report would contain irrelevant information
   B. *correct,* chiefly because a more detailed description of a hydrant should be made by a fireman, not a clerk
   C. *incorrect,* chiefly because the clerk's assignment was to describe the condition of the hydrant and he should give a full explanation
   D. *incorrect,* chiefly because the clerk should include as much information as possible in his report whether or not it is relevant

Questions 9-14.

DIRECTIONS: Questions 9 through 14 are to be answered ONLY on the information contained in the following chart, which shows the number of requisitions filled by Storeroom A during each month of the year.

NUMBER OF REQUISITIONS HANDLED EACH MONTH DURING THE YEAR BY STOREROOM A

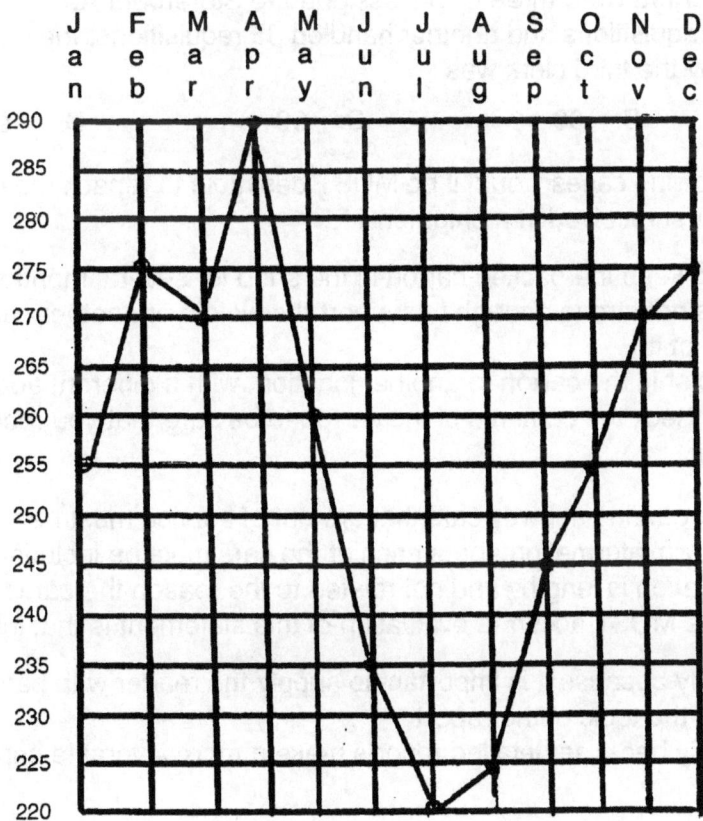

9. According to the above chart, the average number of requisitions handled per month by Storeroom A during the first six months of the year is MOST NEARLY
9.____

    A. 250   B. 260   C. 270   D. 280

10. It is expected that the number of requisitions Storeroom A will handle next year will be 10 percent more than it handled this year.
The number of requisitions Storeroom A is expected to handle next year will MOST likely be
10.____

    A. 2,763   B. 3,070   C. 3,382   D. 3,440

11. The month during which the number of requisitions handled showed the GREATEST decrease from the previous month was
11.____

    A. April   B. May   C. June   D. July

12. During May there were 3 clerks assigned to Storeroom A. One man went on vacation for the month of June and was not replaced.
The number of additional orders handled by each man working in June over the number of orders handled per man in May was MOST NEARLY
12.____

    A. 20   B. 27   C. 32   D. 36

13. During June, July, and August, 8 percent of the requisitions handled were rush orders.
The number of rush orders handled during these three months is MOST NEARLY
13.____

    A. 55   B. 60   C. 65   D. 70

14. During November, there were three clerks assigned to Storeroom A.
If one handled 95 requisitions and another handled 85 requisitions, the number of requisitions handled by the third clerk was
14.____

    A. 70   B. 80   C. 90   D. 100

15. In which of the following cases would it be MOST desirable to repack the contents of a carton which was just received in a shipment?
15.____

    A. You expect to keep the packed carton in the shop for several months.
    B. The carton is not strong enough to support the weight of another carton you want to put on top of it.
    C. You intend to ship the carton to another location, with a different address.
    D. You want to check the contents of the carton to be sure that you received the correct shipment.

16. The daily reports regarding subway cars that are out of service must be prepared in great detail. All known information about each of the cars must be included in the report, even if such information is lengthy and not related to the reason the car is out of service. Of the following, the MOST accurate evaluation of this statement is that it is basically
16.____

    A. *correct*, mainly because it is important to supply the reader with background information about the topic of the report
    B. *correct*, mainly because detailed reports make a more favorable impression upon the reader

C. *incorrect,* mainly because a good report should be as brief as possible and contain only relevant information

D. *incorrect,* mainly because background information about each car should be supplied in a separate report

Questions 17-22.

DIRECTIONS: Questions 17 through 22 are to be answered ONLY on the basis of the information in the chart below.

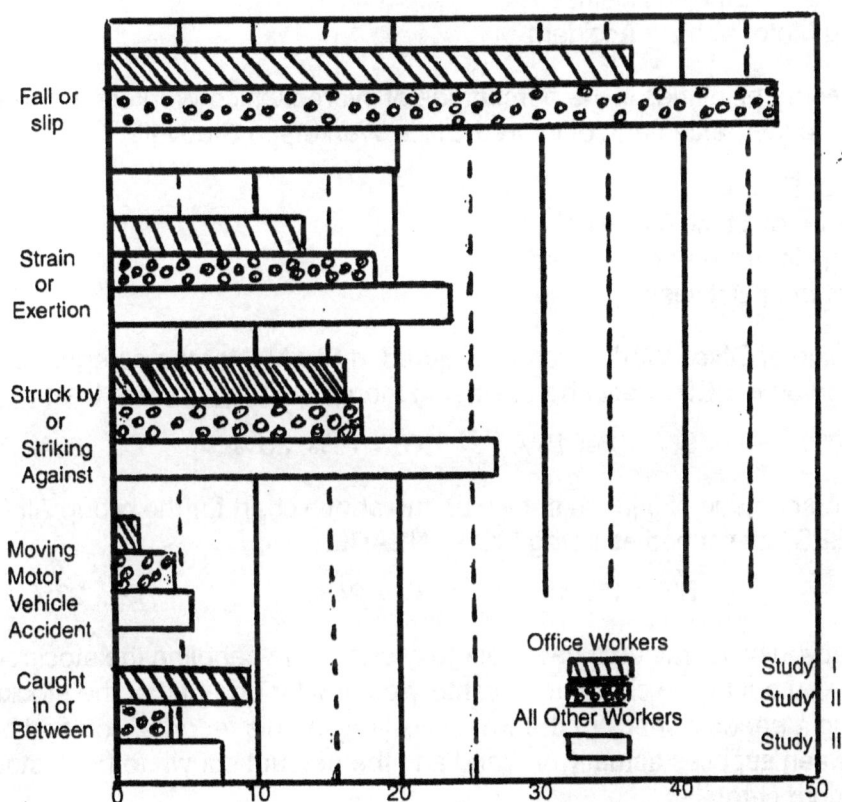

LEADING ACCIDENT TYPES
Office Employees Compared With Other Injured Workers

The above chart shows the results of two studies concerning injuries to office workers. Study I was done only for office workers. The results are represented by ⬛, Study II compared injuries to office workers with injuries to all other workers. In Study II, office workers are represented by ⬛ ; all other workers by ⬜

17. In Study II, in which category of accident was there a 5% difference between the percentage of Office Workers injured and the percentage of All Other Workers injured?   17.____

A. Strain or Exertion
B. Struck by or Striking Against
C. Moving Motor Vehicle Accident
D. Caught In or Between

18. In which category of accident is the average percentage of all Office Workers injured   18.____
closest to the percentage of injuries for All Other Workers?

    A. Fall or Slip
    B. Strain or Exertion
    C. Struck By or Striking Against
    D. Caught In or Between

19. In which category is the percentage of All Other Workers injured MOST NEARLY one-   19.____
half of the average percentage for all Office Workers injured?

    A. Fall or Slip
    B. Strain or Exertion
    C. Struck By or Striking Against
    D. Moving Motor Vehicle Accident

20. In which category of injuries is the percentage of injured Office Workers in Study I shown   20.____
to be closest to the percentage of injured Office Workers in Study II?

    A. Strain or Exertion
    B. Struck By or Striking Against
    C. Moving Motor Vehicle Accident
    D. Caught In or Between

21. The percentage of Office Workers shown injured in Study II for the category of accident   21.____
Strain or Exertion is BEST described as being more than _____ less than _____ .

    A. 5%; 10%   B. 10%; 15%   C. 15%; 20%   D. 20%; 24%

22. The largest percentage of injuries shown on the above chart for the group All Other   22.____
Workers is BEST described as being MOST NEARLY

    A. 18%   B. 21%   C. 24%   D. 27%

23. Suppose that you have trained a new clerk to assist you in handling the stockroom. A few   23.____
weeks later, you put him in charge of inventory control for one-half of the stockroom.
When making a periodic check of the way he is keeping his records, you find quite a difference between supplies actually on hand and the amount shown to be in stock on the
inventory record cards.
Of the following, the BEST action to take in this situation is to

    A. report the clerk to your supervisor because he is not keeping the records properly
    B. tell the clerk that you will order an additional supply of the items to cover the differ-
ence
    C. review the inventory control procedure with the clerk in order to locate the source
of the error
    D. advise the clerk that he is not suited for this job and that you will recommend that
he be transferred

24. You are the clerk in charge of the time cards on which the men in the shop sign in in the   24.____
mornings and sign out in the afternoons. Suppose that one day a co-worker with whom
you are especially friendly asks you to let him sign 15 minutes before the others so that
he can get a seat on the subway.
Of the following, which is the MOST desirable action to take?

A. Go on and let your friend sign out; no one will know about it except the two of you
B. Tell your friend you'll let him sign out this first time, but warn him not to ask again
C. Tell your friend you are going to report him to your supervisor and to his, so he will not try anything like this again
D. Explain to your friend that this is a violation of the rules and that, even though you're friends, you cannot grant his request

25. Suppose that one of the road crew working in a shop receives a great many personal phone calls and constantly requests the clerk to take detailed messages for him. Taking these messages is beginning to take up a lot of the clerk's time.
The BEST thing for the clerk to do under the circumstances is to

    A. tell the man's supervisor that he should put a stop to his men receiving so many personal phone calls
    B. purposely omit or confuse some messages so the worker will stop requesting that he take them
    C. explain to the worker that he cannot spend so much time taking messages because it is interfering with his work
    D. continue to take the messages, but write a report to the worker's supervisor complaining about the phone calls

26. For a six-month period including the previous months, 6 additional mechanics are assigned to work in a shop for a special assignment. The clerk must prepare a vacation schedule for all the men in the shop based on the men's requests and their seniority in the department. Several of the 12 *regulars* in the shop believe they should be given priority, and ask the clerk to do so, even though some of the other men have greater seniority. Under the circumstances, the clerk should

    A. immediately report the *regulars* to their supervisor for trying to break the rules
    B. tell them that, since all the men are assigned to the shop, he must make up the schedule as if they were all *regulars*
    C. try to satisfy the *regulars* since they will be around as co-workers after the other 6 men leave
    D. tell the new men that some of the *regulars* are trying to make trouble for them

27. Assume that you receive a written complaint from an irate vendor shortly after your supervisor has begun his vacation. The supervisor is not expected back for several weeks. The complaint is complex, and you are uncertain about how to reply to it.
Of the following, the BEST course of action for you to take in this situation is to

    A. answer the vendor's complaint as well as you can
    B. assign a clerk in your shop to reply to the vendor's complaint
    C. wait until your supervisor returns from vacation
    D. write to the vendor to tell him that the complaint has been received and that your office is looking into it

28. Suppose that you are a clerk in a transit authority repair shop. A member of the public has called the transit authority to complain about poor ventilation in a subway car, and the call has been transferred to your office. The man demands to speak to the foreman, who is gone for the day to attend a meeting. The man becomes increasingly angry and abusive when you tell him the foreman has gone.
Under the circumstances, the BEST thing for you to do is to

25.____

26.____

27.____

28.____

A. tell the man that if he continues to yell at you you will hang up
B. try to calm the man down and then tell him you will record his complaint and report it to the foreman
C. speak to the man as loudly and rudely as he is speaking to you until he calms down
D. hang up the telephone since the man is not rational and there is no point in talking to him

29. You and a co-worker are both asked by your supervisor to work on a job that requires two men working full-time to complete it on time. You find that your co-worker is *goofing off* and not doing his share of the work.
Of the following, the FIRST thing you should do is to

29.____

A. try to do enough work for two of you, so the job will be finished on time
B. begin to goof off also, so your co-worker will not think he can take advantage of you
C. tell your co-worker that you think he is not doing his share, and that you will have to go to the supervisor if he doesn't straighten out
D. report your co-worker to your supervisor, and tell the supervisor you refuse to continue unless he assigns someone else to work with you

Questions 30-33.

DIRECTIONS: Questions 30 through 33 are to be answered on the basis of the information in the report below.

To: Chief, Division X
From: Mrs. Helen Jones, Clerk
Subject: Accident Involving Two Employees, Mr. John Smith and Mr. Robert Brown

On February 15, Mr. Smith and Mr. Brown were both injured in an accident occurring in the shop at 10 Long Road. No one was in the area of the accident other than Mr. Smith and Mr. Brown. Both of these employees described the following circumstances:

1. Mr. Brown saw the largest tool on the wall begin to fall from where it was hanging and ran up to push Mr. Smith out of the way and to prevent the tool from falling, if possible.
2. Mr. Smith was standing near the wall under some tools which were hanging on nails in the wall.
3. Mr. Brown was standing a few steps from the wall.
4. Mr. Brown stepped toward Mr. Smith, who was on the floor and away from the falling tool. He tripped and fell over a piece of equipment on the floor.
5. Mr. Brown pushed Mr. Smith who slipped on some grease on the floor and fell to the side, out of the way of the falling tool.
6. Mr. Brown tried to avoid Mr. Smith as he fell. In so doing, he fell against some pipes which were leaning against the wall. The pipes fell on both Mr. Brown and Mr. Smith.

Mr. Smith and Mr. Brown were both badly bruised and shaken. They were sent to the General Hospital to determine if any bones were broken. The office was later notified that neither employee was seriously hurt.

Since the accident, matters relating to safety and accident prevention around the shop have occupied the staff. There have been a number of complaints about the location of tools and equipment. Several employees are reluctant to work in the shop unless conditions are improved. Please advise as to the best way to handle this situation.

30. The one of the following which it is MOST important to add to the above memorandum is   30._____

    A. a signature line
    B. a transmittal note
    C. the date of the memo
    D. the initials of the typist

31. The MOST logical order in which to list the circumstances relative to the accident is   31._____

    A. as shown (1, 2, 3, 4, 5, 6)
    B. 2, 3, 1, 5, 4, 6
    C. 1, 5, 4, 6, 3, 2
    D. 3, 2, 4, 6, 1, 5

32. The one of the following which does NOT properly belong with the rest of the memorandum is   32._____

    A. the first section of paragraph 1
    B. the list of circumstances
    C. paragraph 2
    D. paragraph 3

33. According to the information in the memorandum, the BEST description of the subject is   33._____

    A. effect of accident on work output of the division
    B. description of accident involving Mr. Smith and Mr. Brown
    C. recommendations on how to avoid future accidents
    D. safety and accident control in the shop

34. The items of stock which should usually be issued FIRST are those which   34._____

    A. are of best quality
    B. are of poorest quality
    C. have been longest in the storeroom
    D. are not being stored any more

35. If all the new stock of a certain item will not fit on the shelf where the old stock is stored, it would usually be BEST to   35._____

    A. store some of the stock in a new location
    B. store the excess stock in the aisle near the shelf
    C. keep the new stock in the receiving area until the old stock is issued
    D. move all the stock to a new location

36. The MAJOR purpose of maintaining an adequate inventory is to

    A. prevent supply shortages
    B. reduce waste of storage space
    C. increase the dollar value of the organization
    D. provide enough jobs for stockmen

36.____

37. The term *This Side Up* is MOST appropriate on a carton containing

    A. canned food   B. boxes of paper clips
    C. clothing   D. a typewriter

37.____

38. Storeroom records are essential in order to have a supply of each stock item always available.
What information is it NOT necessary to include in storeroom records?

    A. When to reorder stock items
    B. Required delivery time
    C. Means of transportation of delivery
    D. Sources of stock supply

38.____

39. Assume that you usually order a new supply of tires for your agency's fleet of trucks every 6 months. Just before you place an order, you find out that there is a 10% increase expected in the price of tires during the next 3 months.
Of the following, the BEST action for you to take FIRST is to

    A. automatically order a double supply of tires before the prices are increased in order to save the 10%
    B. ignore the expected price increase because it is only expected, not definite
    C. determine what the storage and other costs for an extra order of tires will be and compare it with the cost of a 10% price increase
    D. wait until the new prices go into effect because the more expensive tires will probably be better quality

39.____

40. Assume that your supervisor asks you to do a certain job of unpacking cartons. He tells you how to do it, but you believe there is a better, faster way.
The MOST advisable course of action for you to take is to

    A. follow your supervisor's orders and unpack the cartons his way, without comment
    B. unpack the cartons your way and then show your supervisor the result
    C. ask your co-workers which way they think is better, and do the job that way
    D. explain your way to your supervisor and then ask him which method you should use

40.____

KEY (CORRECT ANSWERS)

1.	B	11.	B	21.	C	31.	B
2.	C	12.	C	22.	D	32.	D
3.	C	13.	A	23.	C	33.	B
4.	A	14.	C	24.	D	34.	C
5.	D	15.	B	25.	C	35.	A
6.	C	16.	C	26.	B	36.	A
7.	A	17.	A	27.	D	37.	D
8.	C	18.	D	28.	B	38.	C
9.	B	19.	A	29.	C	39.	C
10.	C	20.	B	30.	C	40.	D

RECORD KEEPING
EXAMINATION SECTION
TEST 1

DIRECTIONS: Each question or incomplete statement is followed by several suggested answers or completions. Select the one that BEST answers the question or completes the statement. *PRINT THE LETTER OF THE CORRECT ANSWER IN THE SPACE AT THE RIGHT.*

Questions 1-7.

DIRECTIONS: In answering Questions 1 through 7, use the following master list. For each question, determine where the name would fit on the master list. Each answer choice indicates right before or after the name in the answer choice.

Aaron, Jane
Armstead, Brendan
Bailey, Charles
Dent, Ricardo
Grant, Mark
Mars, Justin
Methieu, Justine
Parker, Cathy
Sampson, Suzy
Thomas, Heather

1. Schmidt, William
   A. Right before Cathy Parker
   B. Right after Heather Thomas
   C. Right after Suzy Sampson
   D. Right before Ricardo Dent

   1.____

2. Asanti, Kendall
   A. Right before Jane Aaron
   B. Right after Charles Bailey
   C. Right before Justine Methieu
   D. Right after Brendan Armstead

   2.____

3. O'Brien, Daniel
   A. Right after Justine Methieu
   B. Right before Jane Aaron
   C. Right after Mark Grant
   D. Right before Suzy Sampson

   3.____

4. Marrow, Alison
   A. Right before Cathy Parker
   B. Right before Justin Mars
   C. Right after Mark Grant
   D. Right after Heather Thomas

   4.____

5. Grantt, Marissa
   A. Right before Mark Grant
   B. Right after Mark Grant
   C. Right after Justin Mars
   D. Right before Suzy Sampson

   5.____

6. Thompson, Heath   6.____
   A. Right after Justin Mars   B. Right before Suzy Sampson
   C. Right after Heather Thomas   D. Right before Cathy Parker

DIRECTIONS: Before answering Question 7, add in all of the names from Questions 1 through 6. Then fit the name in alphabetical order based on the new list.

7. Francisco, Mildred   7.____
   A. Right before Mark Grant   B. Right after Marissa Grantt
   C. Right before Alison Marrow   D. Right after Kendall Asanti

Questions 8-10.

DIRECTIONS: In answering Questions 8 through 10, compare each pair of names and addresses. Indicate whether they are the same or different in any way.

8. William H. Pratt, J.D.   William H. Pratt, J.D.   8.____
   Attourney at Law   Attorney at Law
   A. No differences   B. 1 difference
   C. 2 differences   D. 3 differences

9. 1303 Theater Drive,; Apt. 3-B   1330 Theatre Drive,; Apt. 3-B   9.____
   A. No differences   B. 1 difference
   C. 2 differences   D. 3 differences

10. Petersdorff, Briana and Mary   Petersdorff, Briana and Mary   10.____
   A. No differences   B. 1 difference
   C. 2 differences   D. 3 differences

11. Which of the following words, if any, are misspelled?   11.____
   A. Affordable   B. Circumstansial
   C. Legalese   D. None of the above

Questions 12-13.

DIRECTIONS: Questions 12 and 13 are to be answered on the basis of the following table.

Standardized Test Results for High School Students in District #1230

	English	Math	Science	Reading
High School 1	21	22	15	18
High School 2	12	16	13	15
High School 3	16	181	21	17
High School 4	19	14	15	16

The scores for each high school in the district were averaged out and listed for each subject tested. Scores of 0-10 are significantly below College Readiness Standards. 11-15 are below College Readiness, 16-20 meet College Readiness, and 21-25 are above College Readiness.

12. If the high schools need to meet or exceed in at least half the categories
in order to NOT be considered "at risk," which schools are considered "at risk"?   12.____
   A. High School 2   B. High School 3
   C. High School 4   D. Both A and C

13. What percentage of subjects did the district as a whole meet or exceed   13.____
College Readiness standards?
   A. 25%   B. 50%   C. 75%   D. 100%

Questions 14-15.

DIRECTIONS: Questions 14 and 15 are to be answered on the basis of the following
information.

You have seven employees working as a part of your team: Austin, Emily, Jeremy,
Christina, Martin, Harriet, and Steve. You have just sent an e-mail informing them that
there will be a mandatory training session next week. To ensure that work still gets done,
you are offering the training twice during the week: once on Tuesday and also on
Thursday. This way half the employees will still be working while the other half attend the
training. The only other issue is that Jeremy doesn't work on Tuesdays and Harriet
doesn't work on Thursdays due to compressed work schedules.

14. Which of the following is a possible attendance roster for the first training   14.____
session?
   A. Emily, Jeremy, Steve   B. Steve, Christina, Harriet
   C. Harriet, Jeremy, Austin   D. Steve, Martin, Jeremy

15. If Harriet, Christina, and Steve attend the training session on Tuesday, which   15.____
of the following is a possible roster for Thursday's training session?
   A. Jeremy, Emily, and Austin   B. Emily, Martin, and Harriet
   C. Austin, Christina, and Emily   D. Jeremy, Emily, and Steve

Questions 16-20.

DIRECTIONS: In answering Questions 16 through 20, you will be given a word and will need
to choose the answer choice that is MOST similar or different to the word.

16. Which word means the SAME as *annual*?   16.____
   A. Monthly   B. Usually   C. Yearly   D. Constantly

17. Which word means the SAME as *effort*?   17.____
   A. Energy   B. Equate   C. Cherish   D. Commence

18. Which word means the OPPOSITE of *forlorn*?   18.____
   A. Neglected   B. Lethargy   C. Optimistic   D. Astonished

19. Which word means the SAME as *risk*?   19.____
   A. Admire   B. Hazard   C. Limit   D. Hesitant

20. Which word means the OPPOSITE of *translucent*?
    A. Opaque   B. Transparent   C. Luminous   D. Introverted

20.____

21. Last year, Jamie's annual salary was $50,000. Her boss called her today
    to inform her that she would receive a 20% raise for the upcoming year. How
    much more money will Jamie receive next year?
    A. $60,000   B. $10,000   C. $1,000   D. $51,000

21.____

22. You and a co-worker work for a temp hiring agency as part of their office
    staff. You both are given 6 days off per month. How many days off are you
    and your co-worker given in a year?
    A. 24   B. 72   C. 144   D. 48

22.____

23. If Margot makes $34,000 per year and she works 40 hours per week for
    all 52 weeks, what is her hourly rate?
    A. $16.34/hour   B. $17.00/hour   C. $15.54/hour   D. $13.23/hour

23.____

24. How many dimes are there in $175.00?
    A. 175   B. 1,750   C. 3,500   D. 17,500

24.____

25. If Janey is three times as old as Emily, and Emily is 3, how old is Janey?
    A. 6   B. 9   C. 12   D. 15

25.____

KEY (CORRECT ANSWERS)

1.	C		11.	B
2.	D		12.	A
3.	A		13.	D
4.	B		14.	B
5.	B		15.	A
6.	C		16.	C
7.	A		17.	A
8.	B		18.	C
9.	C		19.	B
10.	A		20.	A

21.	B
22.	C
23.	A
24.	B
25.	B

TEST 2

DIRECTIONS: Each question or incomplete statement is followed by several suggested answers or completions. Select the one that BEST answers the question or completes the statement. *PRINT THE LETTER OF THE CORRECT ANSWER IN THE SPACE AT THE RIGHT.*

Questions 1-6.

DIRECTIONS: Questions 1 through 6 are to be answered on the basis of the following information.

item	name of item to be ordered
quantity	minimum number that can be ordered
beginning amount	amount in stock at start of month
amount received	amount receiving during month
ending amount	amount in stock at end of month
amount used	amount used during month
amount to order	will need at least as much of each item as used in the previous month
unit price	cost of each unit of an item
total price	total price for the order

Item	Quantity	Beginning	Received	Ending	Amount Used	Amount to Order	Unit Price	Total Price
Pens	10	22	10	8	24	20	$0.11	$2.20
Spiral notebooks	8	30	13	12			$0.25	
Binder clips	2 boxes	3 boxes	1 box	1 box			$1.79	
Sticky notes	3 packs	12 packs	4 packs	2 packs			$14.29	
Dry erase markers	1 pack (dozen)	34 markers	8 markers	40 markers			$16.49	
Ink cartridges (printer)	1 cartridge	3 cartridges	1 cartridge	2 cartridges			$79.99	
Folders	10 folders	25 folders	15 folders	10 folders			$1.08	

1. How many packs of sticky notes were used during the month?   1.____
   A. 16   B. 10   C. 12   D. 14

2. How many folders need to be ordered for next month?   2.____
   A. 15   B. 20   C. 30   D. 40

3. What is the total price of notebooks that you will need to order?   3.____
   A. $6.00   B. $0.25   C. $4.50   D. $2.75

4. Which of the following will you spend the second most money on?   4.____
   A. Ink cartridges   B. Dry erase markers
   C. Sticky notes   D. Binder clips

5. How many packs of dry erase markers should you order?   5.____
   A. 1   B. 8   C. 12   D. 0

6.   What will be the total price of the file folders you order?   6.____
        A. $20.16   B. $2.16   C. $1.08   D. $4.32

Questions 7-11.

DIRECTIONS: Questions 7 through 11 are to be answered on the basis of the following table.

Number of Car Accidents, By Location and Cause, for 2014						
	Location 1		Location 2		Location 3	
Cause	Number	Percent	Number	Percent	Number	Percent
Severe Weather	10		25		30	
Excessive Speeding	20	40	5		10	
Impaired Driving	15		15	25	8	
Miscellaneous	5		15		2	4
TOTALS	50	100	60	100	50	100

7.   Which of the following is the third highest cause of accidents for all three   7.____
        locations?
        A. Severe Weather   B. Impaired Driving
        C. Miscellaneous   D. Excessive Speeding

8.   The average number of Severe Weather accidents per week at Location 3   8.____
        for the year (52 weeks) was MOST NEARLY
        A. 0.57   B. 30   C. 1   D. 1.25

9.   Which location had the LARGEST percentage of accidents caused by   9.____
        Impaired Driving?
        A. 1   B. 2   C. 3   D. Both A and B

10.   If one-third of the accidents at all three locations resulted in at least one   10.____
        fatality, what is the LEAST amount of deaths caused by accidents last year?
        A. 60   B. 106   C. 66   D. 53

11.   What is the percentage of accidents caused by miscellaneous means from   11.____
        all three locations in 2014?
        A. 5%   B. 10%   C. 13%   D. 25%

12.   How many pairs of the following groups of letters are exactly alike?   12.____
            ACDOBJ   ACDBOJ
            HEWBWR   HEWRWB
            DEERVS   DEERVS
            BRFQSX   BRFQSX
            WEYRVB   WEYRVB
            SPQRZA   SQRPZA

        A. 2   B. 3   C. 4   D. 5

Questions 13-19.

DIRECTIONS: Questions 13 through 19 are to be answered on the basis of the following
information.

In 2012, the most current information on the American population was finished. The
population was compiled by 200 people from each of the 50 states. The territory of Puerto Rico,
a sovereign of the United States, had 25 people assigned to compile data. In February of 2010,
each state began collecting information. In Puerto Rico, data collection finished by January 31st,
2011, while the United States finished on June 30, 2012. Each volunteer gathered data on the
population of each state or sovereign. When the information was compiled, each volunteer had
to send their information to the nation's capital, Washington, D.C. Each worker worked 20
hours per month and put together 10 reports per month. After the data was compiled in total, 50
people reviewed the data and worked from January 2012 to December 2012.

13. How many reports were generated from February 2010 to April 2010 in Illinois   13._____
     and Ohio?
     A. 3,000   B. 6,000   C. 12,000   D. 15,000

14. How many workers in total were collecting data in January 2012?   14._____
     A. 200   B. 25   C. 225   D. 0

15. How many reports were put together in May 2012?   15._____
     A. 2,000   B. 50,000   C. 100,000   D. 100,250

16. How many hours did the Puerto Rican volunteers work in the fall   16._____
     (September-November)?
     A. 60   B. 500   C. 1,500   D. 0

17. How many workers were there in February 2011?   17._____
     A. 25   B. 200   C. 225   D. 250

18. What was the total amount of hours worked in July 2010?   18._____
     A. 500   B. 4,000   C. 4,500   D. 5,000

19. How many reviewers worked in January 2013?   19._____
     A. 75   B. 50   C. 0   D. 25

20. John has to file 10 documents per shelf. How many documents would it   20._____
     take for John to fill 40 shelves?
     A. 40   B. 400   C. 4,500   D. 5,000

21. Jill wants to travel from New York City to Los Angeles by bike, which   21._____
     is approximately 2,772 miles. How many miles per day would Jill need to
     average if she wanted to complete the trip in 4 weeks?
     A. 100   B. 89   C. 99   D. 94

22. If there are 24 CPU's and only 7 monitors, how many more monitors do you need to have the same amount of monitors as CPU's?
    A. Not enough information
    C. 31
    B. 17
    D. 0

22.____

23. If Gerry works 5 days a week and 8 hours each day, and John works 3 days a week and 10 hours each day, how many more hours per year will Gerry work than John?
    A. They work the same amount of hours.
    B. 450
    C. 520
    D. 832

23.____

24. Jimmy gets transferred to a new office. The new office has 25 employees, but only 16 are there due to a blizzard. How many coworkers was Jimmy able to meet on his first day?
    A. 16
    B. 25
    C. 9
    D. 7

24.____

25. If you do a fundraiser for charities in your area and raise $500 total, how much would you give to each charity if you were donating equal amounts to 3 of them?
    A. $250.00
    B. $167.77
    C. $50.00
    D. $111.11

25.____

KEY (CORRECT ANSWERS)

1.	D		11.	C
2.	B		12.	B
3.	A		13.	C
4.	C		14.	A
5.	D		15.	A
6.	B		16.	C
7.	D		17.	B
8.	A		18.	C
9.	A		19.	C
10.	D		20.	B

21.	C
22.	B
23.	C
24.	A
25.	B

TEST 3

DIRECTIONS: Each question or incomplete statement is followed by several suggested answers or completions. Select the one that BEST answers the question or completes the statement. *PRINT THE LETTER OF THE CORRECT ANSWER IN THE SPACE AT THE RIGHT.*

Questions 1-3.

DIRECTIONS: In answering Questions 1 through 3, choose the correctly spelled word.

1. A. allusion   B. alusion   C. allusien   D. allution   1.____

2. A. altitude   B. alltitude   C. atlitude   D. altlitude   2.____

3. A. althogh   B. allthough   C. althrough   D. although   3.____

Questions 4-9.

DIRECTIONS: In answering Questions 4 through 9, choose the answer that BEST completes the analogy.

4. Odometer is to mileage as compass is to   4.____
    A. speed   B. needle   C. hiking   D. direction

5. Marathon is to race as hibernation is to   5.____
    A. winter   B. dream   C. sleep   D. bear

6. Cup is to coffee as bowl is to   6.____
    A. dish   B. spoon   C. food   D. soup

7. Flow is to river as stagnant is to   7.____
    A. pool   B. rain   C. stream   D. canal

8. paw is to cat as hoof is to   8.____
    A. lamb   B. horse   C. lion   D. elephant

9. Architect is to building as sculptor is to   9.____
    A. museum   B. chisel   C. stone   D. statue

Questions 10-14.

DIRECTIONS: Questions 10 through 14 are to be answered on the basis of the following graph.

Population of Carroll City Broken Down by Age and Gender			
(In Thousands) Age	Female	Male	Total
Under 15	60	60	80
15-23		22	
24-33		20	44
34-43	13	18	31
44-53	20		67
64 and Over	65	65	130
TOTAL	225	237	422

10. How many people in the city are between the ages of 15-23?   10.____
    A. 70   B. 46,000   C. 70,000   D. 225,000

11. Approximately what percentage of the total population of the city was   11.____
female aged 24-33?
    A. 10%   B. 5%   C. 15%   D. 25%

12. If 33% of the males have a job and 55% of females don't have a job,   12.____
which of the following statements is TRUE?
    A. Males have 2,251 more jobs than females.
    B. Females have 44,760 more jobs than males.
    C. Females have 22,251 more jobs than males.
    D. None of the above statements are true.

13. How many females between the ages of 15-23 live in Carroll City?   13.____
    A. 67,000   B. 24,000   C. 48,000   D. 91,000

14. Assume all males 44-53 living in Carroll city are employed. If two-thirds   14.____
of males age 44-53 work jobs outside of Carroll City, how many work within city
limits?
    A. 31,333
    B. 15,667
    C. 47,000
    D. Cannot answer the question with the information provided

Questions 15-16.

DIRECTIONS: Questions 15 and 16 are labeled as shown. Alphabetize them for filing. Choose the answer that correctly shows the order.

15. (1) AED
    (2) OOS
    (3) FOA
    (4) DOM
    (5) COB

    A. 2-5-4-3-2   B. 1-4-5-2-3   C. 1-5-4-2-3   D. 1-5-4-3-2

15.____

16. Alphabetize the names of the people. Last names are given last.
    (1) Lindsey Jamestown
    (2) Jane Alberta
    (3) Ally Jamestown
    (4) Allison Johnston
    (5) Lyle Moreno

    A. 2-1-3-4-5   B. 3-4-2-1-5   C. 2-3-1-4-5   D. 4-3-2-1-5

16.____

17. Which of the following words is misspelled?
    A. disgust   B. whisper
    C. vocale   D. none of the above

17.____

Questions 18-21.

DIRECTIONS: Questions 18 through 21 are to be answered on the basis of the following list of employees.

Robertson, Aaron
Bacon, Gina
Jerimiah, Trace
Gillette, Stanley
Jacks, Sharon

18. Which employee name would come in third in alphabetized list?
    A. Robertson, Aaron   B. Jerimiah, Trace
    C. Gillette, Stanley   D. Jacks, Sharon

18.____

19. Which employee's first name starts with the letter in the alphabet that is five letters after the first letter of their last name?
    A. Jerimiah, Trace   B. Bacon, Gina
    C. Jacks, Sharon   D. Gillette, Stanley

19.____

20. How many employees have last names that are exactly five letters long?
    A. 1   B. 2   C. 3   D. 4

20.____

21. How many of the employees have either a first or last name that starts   21.____
     with the letter "G"?
     A. 1   B. 2   C. 4   D. 5

Questions 22-25.

DIRECTIONS: Questions 22 through 25 are to be answered on the basis of the following
             chart.

Bicycle Sales (Model #34JA32)							
Country	May	June	July	August	September	October	Total
Germany	34	47	45	54	56	60	296
Britain	40	44	36	47	47	46	260
Ireland	37	32	32	32	34	33	200
Portugal	14	14	14	16	17	14	89
Italy	29	29	28	31	29	31	177
Belgium	22	24	24	26	25	23	144
Total	176	198	179	206	208	207	1166

22. What percentage of the overall total was sold to the German importer?   22.____
     A. 25.3%   B. 22%   C. 24.1%   D. 23%

23. What percentage of the overall total was sold in September?   23.____
     A. 24.1%   B. 25.6%   C. 17.9%   D. 24.6%

24. What is the average number of units per month imported into Belgium over   24.____
     the first four months shown?
     A. 26   B. 20   C. 24   D. 31

25. If you look at the three smallest importers, what is their total import   25.____
     percentage?
     A. 35.1%   B. 37.1%   C. 40%   D. 28%

KEY (CORRECT ANSWERS)

1.	A		11.	B
2.	A		12.	C
3.	D		13.	C
4.	D		14.	B
5.	C		15.	D
6.	D		16.	C
7.	A		17.	D
8.	B		18.	D
9.	D		19.	B
10.	C		20.	B

21.	B
22.	A
23.	C
24.	C
25.	A

TEST 4

DIRECTIONS: Each question or incomplete statement is followed by several suggested answers or completions. Select the one that BEST answers the question or completes the statement. *PRINT THE LETTER OF THE CORRECT ANSWER IN THE SPACE AT THE RIGHT.*

Questions 1-6.

DIRECTIONS: In answering Questions 1 through 6, choose the sentence that represents the BEST example of English grammar.

1. A. Joey and me want to go on a vacation next week.   1.____
   B. Gary told Jim he would need to take some time off.
   C. If turning six years old, Jim's uncle would teach Spanish to him.
   D. Fax a copy of your resume to Ms. Perez and me.

2. A. Jerry stood in line for almost two hours.   2.____
   B. The reaction to my engagement was less exciting than I thought it would be.
   C. Carlos and me have done great work on this project.
   D. Two parts of the speech needs to be revised before tomorrow.

3. A. Arriving home, the alarm was tripped.   3.____
   B. Jonny is regarded as a stand up guy, a responsible parent, and he doesn't give up until a task is finished.
   C. Each employee must submit a drug test each month.
   D. One of the documents was incinerated in the explosion.

4. A. As soon as my parents get home, I told them I finished all of my chores.   4.____
   B. I asked my teacher to send me my missing work, check my absences, and how did I do on my test.
   C. Matt attempted to keep it concealed from Jenny and me.
   D. If Mary or him cannot get work done on time, I will have to split them up.

5. A. Driving to work, the traffic report warned him of an accident on Highway 47.   5.____
   B. Jimmy has performed well this season.
   C. Since finishing her degree, several job offers have been given to Cam.
   D. Our boss is creating unstable conditions for we employees.

6. A. The thief was described as a tall man with a wiry mustache weighing approximately 150 pounds.   6.____
   B. She gave Patrick and I some more time to finish our work.
   C. One of the books that he ordered was damaged in shipping.
   D. While talking on the rotary phone, the car Jim was driving skidded off the road.

Questions 7-9.

DIRECTIONS: Questions 7 through 9 are to be answered on the basis of the following graph.

Ice Lake Frozen Flight (2002-2013)		
Year	Number of Participants	Temperature (Fahrenheit)
2002	22	4°
2003	50	33°
2004	69	18°
2005	104	22°
2006	108	24°
2007	288	33°
2008	173	9°
2009	598	39°
2010	698	26°
2011	696	30°
2012	777	28°
2013	578	32°

7.   Which two year span had the LARGEST difference between temperatures?   7.____
     A. 2002 and 2003   B. 2011 and 2012
     C. 2008 and 2009   D. 2003 and 2004

8.   How many total people participated in the years after the temperature   8.____
     reached at least 29°?
     A. 2,295   B. 1,717   C. 2,210   D. 4,543

9.   In 2007, the event saw 288 participants, while in 2008 that number   9.____
     dropped to 173. Which of the following reasons BEST explains the drop in
     participants?
     A. The event had not been going on that long and people didn't know about
         it.
     B. The lake water wasn't cold enough to have people jump in.
     C. The temperature was too cold for many people who would have normally
         participated.
     D. None of the above reasons explain the drop in participants.

10. In the following list of numbers, how many times does 4 come just after 2   10.____
     when 2 comes just after an odd number?
     23652476538986324885572486392424
     A. 2   B. 3   C. 4   D. 5

11. Which choice below lists the letter that is as far after B as S is after N in   11.____
     the alphabet?
     A. G   B. H   C. I   D. J

Questions 12-15.

DIRECTIONS: Questions 12 through 15 are to be answered on the basis of the following directory and list of changes.

Directory		
Name	Emp. Type	Position
Julie Taylor	Warehouse	Packer
James King	Office	Administrative Assistant
John Williams	Office	Salesperson
Ray Moore	Warehouse	Maintenance
Kathleen Byrne	Warehouse	Supervisor
Amy Jones	Office	Salesperson
Paul Jonas	Office	Salesperson
Lisa Wong	Warehouse	Loader
Eugene Lee	Office	Accountant
Bruce Lavine	Office	Manager
Adam Gates	Warehouse	Packer
Will Suter	Warehouse	Packer
Gary Lorper	Office	Accountant
Jon Adams	Office	Salesperson
Susannah Harper	Office	Salesperson

Directory Updates:
- Employee e-mail address will adhere to the following guidelines: lastnamefirstname@apexindustries.com (ex. Susannah Harper is harpersusannah@apexindustries.com). Currently, employees in the warehouse share one e-mail, distribution@apexindustries.com.
- The "Loader" position was now be referred to as "Specialist I"
- Adam Gates has accepted a Supervisor position within the Warehouse and is no longer a Packer. All warehouses employees report to the two Supervisors and all office employees report to the Manager.

12.   Amy Jones tried to send an e-mail to Adam Gates, but it wouldn't send.   Which of the following offers the BEST explanation?
   A. Amy put Adam's first name first and then his last name.
   B. Adam doesn't check his e-mail, so he wouldn't know if he received the e-mail or not.
   C. Adam does not have his own e-mail.
   D. Office employees are not allowed to send e-mails to each other.

12.____

13.   How many Packers currently work for Apex Industries?
   A. 2   B. 3   C. 4   D. 5

13.____

14.   What position does Lisa Wong currently hold?
   A. Specialist I   B. Secretary
   C. Administrative Assistant   D. Loader

14.____

15. If an employee wanted to contact the office manager, which of the
    following e-mails should the e-mail be sent to?
    A. officemanager@apexindustries.com
    B. brucelavine@apexindustries.com
    C. lavinebruce@apexindustries.com
    D. distribution@apexindustries.com

15.____

Questions 16-19.

DIRECTIONS: In answering Questions 16 through 19, compare the three names, numbers or
              addresses.

16. Smiley Yarnell   Smiley Yarnel   Smily Yarnell   16.____
    A. All three are exactly alike.
    B. The first and second are exactly alike.
    C. The second and third are exactly alike.
    D. All three are different.

17. 1583 Theater Drive   1583 Theater Drive   1583 Theatre Drive   17.____
    A. All three are exactly alike.
    B. The first and second are exactly alike.
    C. The second and third are exactly alike.
    D. All three are different.

18. 3341893212   3341893212   3341893212   18.____
    A. All three are exactly alike.
    B. The first and second are exactly alike.
    C. The second and third are exactly alike.
    D. All three are different.

19. Douglass Watkins   Douglas Watkins   Douglass Watkins   19.____
    A. All three are exactly alike.
    B. The first and third are exactly alike.
    C. The second and third are exactly alike.
    D. All three are different.

Questions 20-24.

DIRECTIONS: In answering Questions 20 through 24, you will be presented with a word.
              Choose the synonym that BEST represents the word in question.

20. Flexible   20.____
    A. delicate   B. inflammable   C. strong   D. pliable

21. Alternative   21.____
    A. choice   B. moderate   C. lazy   D. value

22. Corroborate
    A. examine   B. explain   C. verify   D. explain

22.____

23. Respiration
    A. recovery   B. breathing   C. sweating   D. selfish

23.____

24. Negligent
    A. lazy   B. moderate   C. hopeless   D. lax

24.____

25. Plumber is to Wrench as Painter is to
    A. pipe   B. shop   C. hammer   D. brush

25.____

KEY (CORRECT ANSWERS)

1.	D		11.	A
2.	A		12.	C
3.	D		13.	A
4.	C		14.	A
5.	B		15.	C
6.	C		16.	D
7.	C		17.	B
8.	B		18.	A
9.	C		19.	B
10.	C		20.	D

21.	A
22.	C
23.	B
24.	D
25.	D

CLERICAL ABILITIES

EXAMINATION SECTION
TEST 1

DIRECTIONS: Each question or incomplete statement is followed by several suggested answers or completions. Select the one that BEST answers the question or completes the statement. *PRINT THE LETTER OF THE CORRECT ANSWER IN THE SPACE AT THE RIGHT.*

Questions 1-4.

DIRECTIONS: Questions 1 through 4 are to be answered on the basis of the information given below.

The most commonly used filing system and the one that is easiest to learn is alphabetical filing. This involves putting records in an A to Z order, according to the letters of the alphabet. The name of a person is filed by using the following order: first, the surname or last name; second, the first name; third, the middle name or middle initial. For example, *Henry C. Young* is filed under *Y* and thereafter under *Young, Henry C.* The name of a company is filed in the same way. For example, *Long Cabinet Co.* is filed under *L*, while *John T. Long Cabinet Co.* is filed under *L* and thereafter under *Long., John T. Cabinet Co.*

1. The one of the following which lists the names of persons in the CORRECT alphabetical order is:

    A. Mary Carrie, Helen Carrol, James Carson, John Carter
    B. James Carson, Mary Carrie, John Carter, Helen Carrol
    C. Helen Carrol, James Carson, John Carter, Mary Carrie
    D. John Carter, Helen Carrol, Mary Carrie, James Carson

1._____

2. The one of the following which lists the names of persons in the CORRECT alphabetical order is:

    A. Jones, John C.; Jones, John A.; Jones, John P.; Jones, John K.
    B. Jones, John P.; Jones, John K.; Jones, John C.; Jones, John A.
    C. Jones, John A.; Jones, John C.; Jones, John K.; Jones, John P.
    D. Jones, John K.; Jones, John C.; Jones, John A.; Jones, John P.

2._____

3. The one of the following which lists the names of the companies in the CORRECT alphabetical order is:

    A. Blane Co., Blake Co., Block Co., Blear Co.
    B. Blake Co., Blane Co., Blear Co., Block Co.
    C. Block Co., Blear Co., Blane Co., Blake Co.
    D. Blear Co., Blake Co., Blane Co., Block Co.

3._____

4. You are to return to the file an index card on *Barry C. Wayne Materials and Supplies Co.* Of the following, the CORRECT alphabetical group that you should return the index card to is

    A. A to G   B. H to M   C. N to S   D. T to Z

4._____

Questions 5-10.

DIRECTIONS: In each of Questions 5 through 10, the names of four people are given. For each question, choose as your answer the one of the four names given which should be filed FIRST according to the usual system of alphabetical filing of names, as described in the following paragraph.

In filing names, you must start with the last name. Names are filed in order of the first letter of the last name, then the second letter, etc. Therefore, BAILY would be filed before BROWN, which would be filed before COLT. A name with fewer letters of the same type comes first; i.e., Smith before Smithe. If the last names are the same, the names are filed alphabetically by the first name. If the first name is an initial, a name with an initial would come before a first name that starts with the same letter as the initial. Therefore, I. BROWN would come before IRA BROWN. Finally, if both last name and first name are the same, the name would be filed alphabetically by the middle name, once again an initial coming before a middle name which starts with the same letter as the initial. If there is no middle name at all, the name would come before those with middle initials or names.

Sample Question: A. Lester Daniels
B. William Dancer
C. Nathan Danzig
D. Dan Lester

The last names beginning with D are filed before the last name beginning with L. Since DANIELS, DANCER, and DANZIG all begin with the same three letters, you must look at the fourth letter of the last name to determine which name should be filed first. C comes before I or Z in the alphabet, so DANCER is filed before DANIELS or DANZIG. Therefore, the answer to the above sample question is B.

5. A. Scott Biala
B. Mary Byala
C. Martin Baylor
D. Francis Bauer

5._____

6. A. Howard J. Black
B. Howard Black
C. J. Howard Black
D. John H. Black

6._____

7. A. Theodora Garth Kingston
B. Theadore Barth Kingston
C. Thomas Kingston
D. Thomas T. Kingston

7._____

8. A. Paulette Mary Huerta
B. Paul M. Huerta
C. Paulette L. Huerta
D. Peter A. Huerta

8._____

9.   A. Martha Hunt Morgan   9.____
       B. Martin Hunt Morgan
       C. Mary H. Morgan
       D. Martine H. Morgan

10.   A. James T. Meerschaum   10.____
       B. James M. Mershum
       C. James F. Mearshaum
       D. James N. Meshum

Questions 11-14.

DIRECTIONS: Questions 11 through 14 are to be answered SOLELY on the basis of the following information.

    You are required to file various documents in file drawers which are labeled according to the following pattern:

DOCUMENTS

MEMOS		LETTERS	
File	Subject	File	Subject
84PM1	(A-L)	84PC1	(A-L)
84PM2	(M-Z)	84PC2	(M-Z)

REPORTS		INQUIRIES	
File	Subject	File	Subject
84PR1	(A-L)	84PQ1	(A-L)
84PR2	(M-Z)	84PQ2	(M-Z)

11.   A letter dealing with a burglary should be filed in the drawer labeled   11.____

    A. 84PM1   B. 84PC1   C. 84PR1   D. 84PQ2

12.   A report on Statistics should be found in the drawer labeled   12.____

    A. 84PM1   B. 84PC2   C. 84PR2   D. 84PQ2

13.   An inquiry is received about parade permit procedures. It should be filed in the drawer labeled   13.____

    A. 84PM2   B. 84PC1   C. 84PR1   D. 84PQ2

14.   A police officer has a question about a robbery report you filed.
You should pull this file from the drawer labeled   14.____

    A. 84PM1   B. 84PM2   C. 84PR1   D. 84PR2

Questions 15-22.

DIRECTIONS: Each of Questions 15 through 22 consists of four or six numbered names. For each question, choose the option (A, B, C, or D) which indicates the order in which the names should be filed in accordance with the following filing instructions:
- File alphabetically according to last name, then first name, then middle initial.
- File according to each successive letter within a name.

- When comparing two names in which, the letters in the longer name are identical to the corresponding letters in the shorter name, the shorter name is filed first.
- When the last names are the same, initials are always filed before names beginning with the same letter.

15.   I.   Ralph Robinson
         II. Alfred Ross
         III. Luis Robles
         IV. James Roberts
The CORRECT filing sequence for the above names should be

   A. IV, II, I, III   B. I, IV, III, II
   C. III, IV, I, II   D. IV, I, III, II

15.____

16.   I.   Irwin Goodwin
         II. Inez Gonzalez
         III. Irene Goodman
         IV. Ira S. Goodwin
         V. Ruth I. Goldstein
         VI. M.B. Goodman
The CORRECT filing sequence for the above names should be

   A. V, II, I, IV, III, VI   B. V, II, VI, III, IV, I
   C. V, II, III, VI, IV, I   D. V, II, III, VI, I, IV

16.____

17.   I.   George Allan
         II. Gregory Allen
         III. Gary Allen
         IV. George Allen
The CORRECT filing sequence for the above names should be

   A. IV, III, I, II   B. I, IV, II, III
   C. III, IV, I, II   D. I, III, IV, II

17.____

18.   I.   Simon Kauffman
         II. Leo Kaufman
         III. Robert Kaufmann
         IV. Paul Kauffmann
The CORRECT filing sequence for the above names should be

   A. I, IV, II, III   B. II, IV, III, I
   C. III, II, IV, I   D. I, II, III, IV

18.____

19.   I.   Roberta Williams
         II. Robin Wilson
         III. Roberta Wilson
         IV. Robin Williams
The CORRECT filing sequence for the above names should be

   A. III, II, IV, I   B. I, IV, III, II
   C. I, II, III, IV   D. III, I, II, IV

19.____

20.
    I.   Lawrence Shultz
    II. Albert Schultz
    III. Theodore Schwartz
    IV. Thomas Schwarz
    V. Alvin Schultz
    VI. Leonard Shultz

The CORRECT filing sequence for the above names should be

  A. II, V, III, IV, I, VI
  C. II, V, I, VI, III, IV
  B. IV, III, V, I, II, VI
  D. I, VI, II, V, III, IV

20.____

21.
    I.   McArdle
    II. Mayer
    III. Maletz
    IV. McNiff
    V. Meyer
    VI. MacMahon

The CORRECT filing sequence for the above names should be

  A. I, IV, VI, III, II, V
  C. VI, III, II, I, IV, V
  B. II, I, IV, VI, III, V
  D. VI, III, II, V, I, IV

21.____

22.
    I.   Jack E. Johnson
    II. R.H. Jackson
    III. Bertha Jackson
    IV. J.T. Johnson
    V. Ann Johns
    VI. John Jacobs

The CORRECT filing sequence for the above names should be

  A. II, III, VI, V, IV, I
  C. VI, II, III, I, V, IV
  B. III, II, VI, V, IV, I
  D. III, II, VI, IV, V, I

22.____

Questions 23-30.

DIRECTIONS: The code table below shows 10 letters with matching numbers. For each question, there are three sets of letters. Each set of letters is followed by a set of numbers which may or may not match their correct letter according to the code table. For each question, check all three sets of letters and numbers and mark your answer:
    A. if no pairs are correctly matched
    B. if only one pair is correctly matched
    C. if only two pairs are correctly matched
    D. if all three pairs are correctly matched

CODE TABLE

T	M	V	D	S	P	R	G	B	H
1	2	3	4	5	6	7	8	9	0

Sample Question: TMVDSP - 123456
                           RGBHTM - 789011
                           DSPRGB - 256789

In the sample question above, the first set of numbers correctly matches its set of letters. But the second and third pairs contain mistakes. In the second pair, M is incorrectly matched with number 1. According to the code table, letter M should be correctly matched with number 2. In the third pair, the letter D is incorrectly matched with number 2. According to the code table, letter D should be correctly matched with number 4. Since only one of the pairs is correctly matched, the answer to this sample question is B.

23. RSBMRM 759262
     GDSRVH 845730
     VDBRTM 349713

23._____

24. TGVSDR 183247
     SMHRDP 520647
     TRMHSR 172057

24._____

25. DSPRGM 456782
     MVDBHT 234902
     HPMDBT 062491

25._____

26. BVPTRD 936184
     GDPHMB 807029
     GMRHMV 827032

26._____

27. MGVRSH 283750
     TRDMBS 174295
     SPRMGV 567283

27._____

28. SGBSDM 489542
     MGHPTM 290612
     MPBMHT 269301

28._____

29. TDPBHM 146902
     VPBMRS 369275
     GDMBHM 842902

29._____

30. MVPTBV 236194
     PDRTMB 647128
     BGTMSM 981232

30._____

KEY (CORRECT ANSWERS)

1.	A	11.	B	21.	C
2.	C	12.	C	22.	B
3.	B	13.	D	23.	B
4.	D	14.	D	24.	B
5.	D	15.	D	25.	C
6.	B	16.	C	26.	A
7.	B	17.	D	27.	D
8.	B	18.	A	28.	A
9.	A	19.	B	29.	D
10.	C	20.	A	30.	A

___

TEST 2

DIRECTIONS: Each question or incomplete statement is followed by several suggested answers or completions. Select the one that BEST answers the question or completes the statement. *PRINT THE LETTER OF THE CORRECT ANSWER IN THE SPACE AT THE RIGHT.*

Questions 1-10.

DIRECTIONS: Questions 1 through 10 each consists of two columns, each containing four lines of names, numbers and/or addresses. For each question, compare the lines in Column I with the lines in Column II to see if they match exactly, and mark your answer A, B, C, or D, according to the following instructions:
- A. all four lines match exactly
- B. only three lines match exactly
- C. only two lines match exactly
- D. only one line matches exactly

		COLUMN I	COLUMN II	
1.	I. II. III. IV.	Earl Hodgson 1409870 Shore Ave. Macon Rd.	Earl Hodgson 1408970 Schore Ave. Macon Rd.	1.____
2.	I. II. III. IV.	9671485 470 Astor Court Halprin, Phillip Frank D. Poliseo	9671485 470 Astor Court Halperin, Phillip Frank D. Poliseo	2.____
3.	I. II. III. IV.	Tandem Associates 144-17 Northern Blvd. Alberta Forchi Kings Park, NY 10751	Tandom Associates 144-17 Northern Blvd. Albert Forchi Kings Point, NY 10751	3.____
4.	I. II. III. IV.	Bertha C. McCormack Clayton, MO. 976-4242 New City, NY 10951	Bertha C. McCormack Clayton, MO. 976-4242 New City, NY 10951	4.____
5.	I. II. III. IV.	George C. Morill Columbia, SC 29201 Louis Ingham 3406 Forest Ave.	George C. Morrill Columbia, SD 29201 Louis Ingham 3406 Forest Ave.	5.____
6.	I. II. III. IV.	506 S. Elliott Pl. Herbert Hall 4712 Rockaway Pkway 169 E. 7 St.	506 S. Elliott Pl. Hurbert Hall 4712 Rockaway Pkway 169 E. 7 St.	6.____

	COLUMN I	COLUMN II	
7.	I. 345 Park Ave.	345 Park Pl.	7._____
	II. Colman Oven Corp.	Coleman Oven Corp.	
	III. Robert Conte	Robert Conti	
	IV. 6179846	6179846	
8.	I. Grigori Schierber	Grigori Schierber	8._____
	II. Des Moines, Iowa	Des Moines, Iowa	
	III. Gouverneur Hospital	Gouverneur Hospital	
	IV. 91-35 Cresskill Pl.	91-35 Cresskill Pl.	
9.	I. Jeffery Janssen	Jeffrey Janssen	9._____
	II. 8041071	8041071	
	III. 40 Rockefeller Plaza	40 Rockafeller Plaza	
	IV. 407 6 St.	406 7 St.	
10.	I. 5971996	5871996	10._____
	II. 3113 Knickerbocker Ave.	3113 Knickerbocker Ave.	
	III. 8434 Boston Post Rd.	8424 Boston Post Rd.	
	IV. Penn Station	Penn Station	

Questions 11-14.

DIRECTIONS: Questions 11 through 14 are to be answered by looking at the four groups of names and addresses listed below (I, II, III, and IV) and then finding out the number of groups that have their corresponding numbered lines exactly the same.

GROUP I
Line 1. Richmond General Hospital
Line 2. Geriatric Clinic
Line 3. 3975 Paerdegat St.
Line 4 Loudonville, New York 11538

GROUP II
Richman General Hospital
Geriatric Clinic
3975 Peardegat St.
Londonville, New York 11538

GROUP III
Line 1. Richmond General Hospital
Line 2. Geriatric Clinic
Line 3. 3795 Paerdegat St.
Line 4. Loudonville, New York 11358

GROUP IV
Richmend General Hospital
Geriatric Clinic
3975 Paerdegat St.
Loudonville, New York 11538

11. In how many groups is line one exactly the same?   11._____

    A. Two   B. Three   C. Four   D. None

12. In how many groups is line two exactly the same?   12._____

    A. Two   B. Three   C. Four   D. None

13. In how many groups is line three exactly the same?   13._____

    A. Two   B. Three   C. Four   D. None

14. In how many groups is line four exactly the same?　　　　　　　　　　14.____

    A.　Two　　　　　B.　Three　　　　C.　Four　　　　D.　None

Questions 15-18.

DIRECTIONS:　Each of Questions 15 through 18 has two lists of names and addresses. Each list contains three sets of names and addresses. Check each of the three sets in the list on the right to see if they are the same as the corresponding set in the list on the left. Mark your answers:

    A.　if none of the sets in the right list are the same as those in the left list
    B.　if only one of the sets in the right list is the same as those in the left list
    C.　if only two of the sets in the right list are the same as those in the left list
    D.　if all three sets in the right list are the same as those in the left list

15.
Mary T. Berlinger 2351 Hampton St. Monsey, N.Y. 20117	Mary T. Berlinger 2351 Hampton St. Monsey, N.Y. 20117
Eduardo Benes 473 Kingston Avenue Central Islip, N.Y. 11734	Eduardo Benes 473 Kingston Avenue Central Islip, N.Y. 11734
Alan Carrington Fuchs 17 Gnarled Hollow Road Los Angeles, CA 91635	Alan Carrington Fuchs 17 Gnarled Hollow Road Los Angeles, CA 91685

15.____

16.
David John Jacobson 178 35 St. Apt. 4C New York, N.Y. 00927	David John Jacobson 178 53 St. Apt. 4C New York, N.Y. 00927
Ann-Marie Calonella 7243 South Ridge Blvd. Bakersfield, CA 96714	Ann-Marie Calonella 7243 South Ridge Blvd. Bakersfield, CA 96714
Pauline M. Thompson 872 Linden Ave. Houston, Texas 70321	Pauline M. Thomson 872 Linden Ave. Houston, Texas 70321

16.____

17.
Chester LeRoy Masterton 152 Lacy Rd. Kankakee, Ill. 54532	Chester LeRoy Masterson 152 Lacy Rd. Kankakee, Ill. 54532
William Maloney S. LaCrosse Pla. Wausau, Wisconsin 52146	William Maloney S. LaCross Pla. Wausau, Wisconsin 52146
Cynthia V. Barnes 16 Pines Rd. Greenpoint, Miss. 20376	Cynthia V. Barnes 16 Pines Rd. Greenpoint, Miss. 20376

17.____

18.

Marcel Jean Frontenac 8 Burton On The Water Calender, Me. 01471	Marcel Jean Frontenac 6 Burton On The Water Calender, Me. 01471
J. Scott Marsden 174 S. Tipton St. Cleveland, Ohio	J. Scott Marsden 174 Tipton St. Cleveland, Ohio
Lawrence T. Haney 171 McDonough St. Decatur, Ga. 31304	Lawrence T. Haney 171 McDonough St. Decatur, Ga. 31304

18._____

Questions 19-26.

DIRECTIONS: Each of Questions 19 through 26 has two lists of numbers. Each list contains three sets of numbers. Check each of the three sets in the list on the right to see if they are the same as the corresponding set in the list on the left. Mark your answers:
- A. if none of the sets in the right list are the same as those in the left list
- B. if only one of the sets in the right list is the same as those in the left list
- C. if only two of the sets in the right list are the same as those in the left list
- D. if all three sets in the right list are the same as those in the left list

19. 7354183476
     4474747744
     57914302311

    7354983476
    4474747774
    57914302311

19._____

20. 7143592185
     8344517699
     9178531263

    7143892185
    8344518699
    9178531263

20._____

21. 2572114731
     8806835476
     8255831246

    257214731
    8806835476
    8255831246

21._____

22. 331476853821
     6976658532996
     3766042113715

    331476858621
    6976655832996
    3766042113745

22._____

23. 8806663315
     74477138449
     211756663666

    8806663315
    74477138449
    211756663666

23._____

24. 990006966996
     53022219743
     4171171117717

    99000696996
    53022219843
    4171171177717

24._____

25. 24400222433004
     5300030055000355
     20000075532002022

    24400222433004
    5300030055500355
    20000075532002022

25._____

26. 611166640660001116
     711130011700110073
     26666446664476518

    611166640660001116
    711130011700110073
    26666446664476518

26.____

Questions 27-30.

DIRECTIONS: Questions 27 through 30 are to be answered by picking the answer which is in the correct numerical order, from the lowest number to the highest number, in each question.

27.   A. 44533, 44518, 44516, 44547
       B. 44516, 44518, 44533, 44547
       C. 44547, 44533, 44518, 44516
       D. 44518, 44516, 44547, 44533

27.____

28.   A. 95587, 95593, 95601, 95620
       B. 95601, 95620, 95587, 95593
       C. 95593, 95587, 95601, 95620
       D. 95620, 95601, 95593, 95587

28.____

29.   A. 232212, 232208, 232232, 232223
       B. 232208, 232223, 232212, 232232
       C. 232208, 232212, 232223, 232232
       D. 232223, 232232, 232208, 232212

29.____

30.   A. 113419, 113521, 113462, 113588
       B. 113588, 113462, 113521, 113419
       C. 113521, 113588, 113419, 113462
       D. 113419, 113462, 113521, 113588

30.____

KEY (CORRECT ANSWERS)

1.	C	11.	A	21.	C
2.	B	12.	C	22.	A
3.	D	13.	A	23.	D
4.	A	14.	A	24.	A
5.	C	15.	C	25.	C
6.	B	16.	B	26.	C
7.	D	17.	B	27.	B
8.	A	18.	B	28.	A
9.	D	19.	B	29.	C
10.	C	20.	B	30.	D

NAME AND NUMBER CHECKING

EXAMINATION SECTION
TEST 1

DIRECTIONS: Questions 1 through 17 consist of sets of names and addresses. In each question, the name and address in Column II should be an exact copy of the name and address in Column I.

If there is:
a mistake only in the name, mark your answer A;
a mistake only in the address, mark your answer B;
a mistake in both name and address, mark your answer C;
NO mistake in either name or address, mark your answer D.

SAMPLE QUESTION

Column I

Christina Magnusson
288 Greene Street
New York, N.Y. 10003

Column II

Christina Magnusson
288 Greene Street
New York, N.Y. 10013

Since there is a mistake only in the address (the zip code should be 10003 instead of 10013), the answer to the sample question is B.

COLUMN I	COLUMN II	
1. Ms. Joan Kelly 313 Franklin Ave. Brooklyn, N.Y. 11202	Ms. Joan Klelly 318 Franklin Ave. Brooklyn, N.Y. 11202	1._____
2. Mrs. Eileen Engel 47-24 86 Road Queens, N.Y. 11122	Mrs. Ellen Engel 47-24 86 Road Queens, N.Y. 11122	2._____
3. Marcia Michaels 213 E. 81 St. New York, N.Y. 10012	Marcia Michaels 213 E. 81 St. New York, N.Y. 10012	3._____
4. Rev. Edward J. Smyth 1401 Brandeis Street San Francisco, Calif. 96201	Rev. Edward J. Smyth 1401 Brandies Street San Francisco, Calif. 96201	4._____
5. Alicia Rodriguez 24-68 81 St. Elmhurst, N.Y. 11122	Alicia Rodriguez 2468 81 St. Elmhurst, N.Y. 11122	5._____
6. Ernest Eisemann 21 Columbia St. New York, N.Y. 10007	Ernest Eisermann 21 Columbia St. New York, N.Y. 10007	6._____

Column I	COLUMN II	
7. Mr. & Mrs. George Petersson 87-11 91st Avenue Woodhaven, N.Y. 11421	Mr. & Mrs. George Peterson 87-11 91st Avenue Woodhaven, N.Y. 11421	7.____
8. Mr. Ivan Klebnikov 1848 Newkirk Avenue Brooklyn, N.Y. 11226	Mr. Ivan Klebikov 1848 Newkirk Avenue Brooklyn, N.Y. 11622	8.____
9. Samuel Rothfleisch 71 Pine Street New York, N.Y. 10005	Samuel Rothfleisch 71 Pine Street New York, N.Y. 10005	9.____
10. Mrs. Isabel Tonnessen 198 East 185th Street Bronx, N.Y. 10458	Mrs. Isabel Tonnessen 189 East 185th Street Bronx, N.Y. 10458	10.____
11. Esteban Perez 173 Eighth Street Staten Island, N.Y. 10306	Estaban Perez 173 Eighth Street Staten Island, N.Y. 10306	11.____
12. Esta Wong 141 West 68 St. New York, N.Y. 10023	Esta Wang 141 West 68 St. New York, N.Y. 10023	12.____
13. Dr. Alberto Grosso 3475 12th Avenue Brooklyn, N.Y. 11218	Dr. Alberto Grosso 3475 12th Avenue Brooklyn, N.Y. 11218	13.____
14. Mrs. Ruth Bortlas 482 Theresa Ct. Far Rockaway, N.Y. 11691	Ms. Ruth Bortlas 482 Theresa Ct. Far Rockaway, N.Y. 11169	14.____
15. Mr. & Mrs. Howard Fox 2301 Sedgwick Ave. Bronx, N.Y. 10468	Mr. & Mrs. Howard Fox 231 Sedgwick Ave. Bronx, N.Y. 10468	15.____
16. Miss Marjorie Black 223 East 23 Street New York, N.Y. 10010	Miss Margorie Black 223 East 23 Street New York, N.Y. 10010	16.____
17. Michelle Herman 806 Valley Rd. Old Tappan, N.J. 07675	Michelle Hermann 806 Valley Dr. Old Tappan, N.J. 07675	17.____

KEY (CORRECT ANSWERS)

1.	C	6.	A
2.	A	7.	A
3.	D	8.	C
4.	B	9.	D
5.	B	10.	B

11.	A
12.	A
13.	D
14.	C
15.	B
16.	A
17.	C

———

TEST 2

DIRECTIONS: Questions 1 through 15 are to be answered SOLELY on the instructions given below. *PRINT THE LETTER OF THE CORRECT ANSWER IN THE SPACE AT THE RIGHT.*

INSTRUCTIONS:

In each of the following questions, the 3-line name and address in Column I is the master-list entry, and the 3-line entry in Column 2 is the information to be checked against the master list. If there is one line that does not match, mark your answer A; if there are two lines that do not match, mark your answer B; if all three lines do not match, mark your answer C; if the lines all match exactly, mark your answer D.

SAMPLE QUESTION

Column I
Mark L. Field
11-09 Prince Park Blvd.
Bronx, N.Y. 11402

Column II
Mark L. Field
11-99 Prince Park Way
Bronx, N.Y. 11401

The first lines in each column match exactly. The second lines do not match since 11-09 does not match 11-99; and Blvd. does not match Way. The third lines do not match either since 11402 does not match 11401. Therefore, there are two lines that do not match, and the CORRECT answer is B.

COLUMN I

COLUMN II

1. Jerome A. Jackson
    1243 14th Avenue
    New York, N.Y. 10023

    Jerome A. Johnson
    1234 14th Avenue
    New York, N.Y. 10023

    1.____

2. Sophie Strachtheim
    33-28 Connecticut Ave.
    Far Rockaway, N.Y. 11697

    Sophie Strachtheim
    33-28 Connecticut Ave.
    Far Rockaway, N.Y. 11697

    2.____

3. Elisabeth N.T. Gorrell
    256 Exchange St.
    New York, N.Y. 10013

    Elizabeth N.T. Gorrell
    256 Exchange St.
    New York, N.Y. 10013

    3.____

4. Maria J. Gonzalez
    7516 E. Sheepshead Rd.
    Brooklyn, N.Y. 11240

    Maria J. Gonzalez
    7516 N. Shepshead Rd.
    Brooklyn, N.Y. 11240

    4.____

5. Leslie B. Brautenweiler
    21 57A Seiler Terr.
    Flushing, N.Y. 11367

    Leslie B. Brautenwieler
    21-75A Seiler Terr.
    Flushing, N.J. 11367

    5.____

6. Rigoberto J. Peredes
    157 Twin Towers, #18F
    Tottenville, S.I., N.Y.

    Rigoberto J. Peredes
    157 Twin Towers, #18F
    Tottenville, S.I., N.Y.

    6.____

	COLUMN I	COLUMN II	

7. Pietro F. Albino
P.O. Box 7548
Floral Park, N.Y. 11005

Pietro F. Albina
P.O. Box 7458
Floral Park, N.Y. 11005

7.____

8. Joanne Zimmermann
Bldg. SW, Room 314
532-4601

Joanne Zimmermann
Bldg. SW, Room 314
532-4601

8.____

9. Carlyle Whetstone
Payroll Div.-A, Room 212A
262-5000, ext. 471

Caryle Whetstone
Payroll Div.-A, Room 212A
262-5000, ext. 417

9.____

10. Kenneth Chiang
Legal Council, Room 9745
(201) 416-9100, ext. 17

Kenneth Chiang
Legal Counsel, Room 9745
(201) 416-9100, ext. 17

10.____

11. Ethel Koenig
Personnel Services Division,
Room 433; 635-7572

Ethel Hoenig
Personal Services Division,
Room 433; 635-7527

11.____

12. Joyce Ehrhardt
Office of the Administrator,
Room W56; 387-8706

Joyce Ehrhart
Office of the Administrator,
Room W56; 387-7806

12.____

13. Ruth Lang
EAM Bldg., Room C101
625-2000, ext. 765

Ruth Lang
EAM Bldg., Room C110
625-2000, ext. 765

13.____

14. Anne Marie Ionozzi
Investigations, Room 827
576-4000, ext. 832

Anna Marie Ionozzi
Investigation, Room 827
566-4000, ext. 832

14.____

15. Willard Jameson
Fm C Bldg., Room 687
454-3010

Willard Jamieson
Fm C Bldg., Room 687
454-3010

15.____

KEY (CORRECT ANSWERS)

1.	B		6.	D
2.	D		7.	B
3.	A		8.	D
4.	A		9.	B
5.	C		10.	A

11.	C
12.	B
13.	A
14.	C
15.	A

———

TEST 3

DIRECTIONS: Questions 1 through 10 are to be answered on the basis of the following instructions. *PRINT THE LETTER OF THE CORRECT ANSWER IN THE SPACE AT THE RIGHT.*

INSTRUCTIONS:

For each such set of names, addresses, and numbers listed in Columns I and II, select your answer from the following options:
- A. The names in Columns I and II are different.
- B. The addresses in Columns I and II are different.
- C. The numbers in Columns I and II are different.
- D. The names, addresses, and numbers in Columns I and II are identical.

COLUMN I	COLUMN II	
1. Francis Jones 62 Stately Avenue 96-12446	Francis Jones 62 Stately Avenue 96-21446	1.____
2. Julio Montez 19 Ponderosa Road 56-73161	Julio Montez 19 Ponderosa Road 56-71361	2.____
3. Mary Mitchell 2314 Melbourne Drive 68-92172	Mary Mitchell 2314 Melbourne Drive 68-92172	3.____
4. Harry Patterson 25 Dunne Street 14-33430	Harry Patterson 25 Dunne Street 14-34330	4.____
5. Patrick Murphy 171 West Hosmer Street 93-81214	Patrick Murphy 171 West Hosmer Street 93-18214	5.____
6. August Schultz 816 St. Clair Avenue 53-40149	August Schultz 816 St. Claire Avenue 53-40149	6.____
7. George Taft 72 Runnymede Street 47-04033	George Taft 72 Runnymede Street 47-04023	7.____
8. Angus Henderson 1418 Madison Street 81-76375	Angus Henderson 1418 Madison Street 81-76375	8.____
9. Carolyn Mazur 12 Riverview Road 38-99615	Carolyn Mazur 12 Rivervane ftoad 38-99615	9.____

COLUMN I	COLUMN II	
10. Adele Russell 1725 Lansing Lane 72-91962	Adela Russell 1725 Lansing Lane 72-91962	10.____

KEY (CORRECT ANSWERS)

1.	C	6.	B
2.	C	7.	C
3.	D	8.	D
4.	C	9.	B
5.	C	10.	A

TEST 4

DIRECTIONS: Questions 1 through 20 test how good you are at catching mistakes in typing or printing. In each question, the name and address in Column II should be an exact copy of the name and address in Column I. Mark your answer

    A.   if there is no mistake in either name or address;
    B.   if there is a mistake in both name and address;
    C.   if there is a mistake only in the name;
    D.   if there is a mistake only in the address.

PRINT THE LETTER OF THE CORRECT ANSWER IN THE SPACE AT THE RIGHT.

COLUMN I	COLUMN II	
1. Milos Yanocek 33-60 14 Street Long Island City, N.Y. 11011	Milos Yanocek 33-60 14 Street Long Island City, N.Y. 11001	1.____
2. Alphonse Sabattelo 24 Minnetta Lane New York, N.Y. 10006	Alphonse Sabbattelo 24 Minetta Lane New York, N.Y. 10006	2.____
3. Helen Steam 5 Metropolitan Oval Bronx, N.Y. 10462	Helene Stearn 5 Metropolitan Oval Bronx, N.Y. 10462	3.____
4. Jacob Weisman 231 Francis Lewis Boulevard Forest Hills, N.Y. 11325	Jacob Weisman 231 Francis Lewis Boulevard Forest Hills, N.Y. 11325	4.____
5. Riccardo Fuente 134 West 83 Street New York, N.Y. 10024	Riccardo Fuentes 134 West 88 Street New York, N.Y. 10024	5.____
6. Dennis Lauber 52 Avenue D Brooklyn, N.Y. 11216	Dennis Lauder 52 Avenue D Brooklyn, N.Y. 11216	6.____
7. Paul Cutter 195 Galloway Avenue Staten Island, N.Y. 10356	Paul Cutter 175 Galloway Avenue Staten Island, N.Y. 10365	7.____
8. Sean Donnelly 45-58 41 Avenue Woodside, N.Y. 11168	Sean Donnelly 45-58 41 Avenue Woodside, N.Y. 11168	8.____
9. Clyde Willot 1483 Rockaway Avenue Brooklyn, N.Y. 11238	Clyde Willat 1483 Rockway Avenue Brooklyn, N.Y. 11238	9.____

COLUMN I	COLUMN II	
10. Michael Stanakis 419 Sheriden Avenue Staten Island, N.Y. 10363	Michael Stanakis 419 Sheraden Avenue Staten Island, N.Y. 10363	10.____
11. Joseph DiSilva 63-84 Saunders Road Rego Park, N.Y. 11431	Joseph Disilva 64-83 Saunders Road Rego Park, N.Y. 11431	11.____
12. Linda Polansky 2225 Fenton Avenue Bronx, N.Y. 10464	Linda Polansky 2255 Fenton Avenue Bronx, N.Y. 10464	12.____
13. Alfred Klein 260 Hillside Terrace Staten Island, N.Y. 15545	Alfred Klein 260 Hillside Terrace Staten Island, N.Y. 15545	13.____
14. William McDonnell 504 E. 55 Street New York, N.Y. 10103	William McConnell 504 E. 55 Street New York, N.Y. 10108	14.____
15. Angela Cipolla 41-11 Parson Avenue Flushing, N.Y. 11446	Angela Cipola 41-11 Parsons Avenue Flushing, N.Y. 11446	15.____
16. Julie Sheridan 1212 Ocean Avenue Brooklyn, N.Y. 11237	Julia Sheridan 1212 Ocean Avenue Brooklyn, N.Y. 11237	16.____
17. Arturo Rodriguez 2156 Cruger Avenue Bronx, N.Y. 10446	Arturo Rodrigues 2156 Cruger Avenue Bronx, N.Y. 10446	17.____
18. Helen McCabe 2044 East 19 Street Brooklyn, N.Y. 11204	Helen McCabe 2040 East 19 Street Brooklyn,. N.Y. 11204	18.____
19. Charles Martin 526 West 160 Street New York, N.Y. 10022	Charles Martin 526 West 160 Street New York, N.Y. 10022	19.____
20. Morris Rabinowitz 31 Avenue M Brooklyn, N.Y. 11216	Morris Rabinowitz 31 Avenue N Brooklyn, N.Y. 11216	20.____

KEY (CORRECT ANSWERS)

1.	D		11.	B
2.	B		12.	D
3.	C		13.	A
4.	A		14.	B
5.	B		15.	B
6.	C		16.	C
7.	D		17.	C
8.	A		18.	D
9.	B		19.	A
10.	D		20.	D

TEST 5

DIRECTIONS: In copying the addresses below from Column A to the same line in Column B, an Agent-in-Training made some errors. For Questions 1 through 5, if you find that the Agent made an error in

only one line, mark your answer A;
only two lines, mark your answer B;
only three lines, mark your answer C;
all four lines, mark your answer D.

EXAMPLE

Column A	Column B
24 Third Avenue	24 Third Avenue
5 Lincoln Road	5 Lincoln Street
50 Central Park West	6 Central Park West
37-21 Queens Boulevard	21-37 Queens Boulevard

Since errors were made on only three lines, namely the second, third, and fourth, the COR-RECT answer is C.
PRINT THE LETTER OF THE CORRECT ANSWER IN THE SPACE AT THE RIGHT.

	Column A	Column B	
1.	57-22 Springfield Boulevard	75-22 Springfield Boulevard	1.____
	94 Gun Hill Road	94 Gun Hill Avenue	
	8 New Dorp Lane	8 New Drop Lane	
	36 Bedford Avenue	36 Bedford Avenue	
2.	538 Castle Hill Avenue	538 Castle Hill Avenue	2.____
	54-15 Beach Channel Drive	54-15 Beach Channel Drive	
	21 Ralph Avenue	21 Ralph Avenue	
	162 Madison Avenue	162 Morrison Avenue	
3.	49 Thomas Street	49 Thomas Street	3.____
	27-21 Northern Blvd.	21-27 Northern Blvd.	
	86 125th Street	86 125th Street	
	872 Atlantic Ave.	872 Baltic Ave.	
4.	261-17 Horace Harding Expwy.	261-17 Horace Harding Pkwy.	4.____
	191 Fordham Road	191 Fordham Road	
	6 Victory Blvd.	6 Victoria Blvd.	
	552 Oceanic Ave.	552 Ocean Ave.	
5.	90-05 38th Avenue	90-05 36th Avenue	5.____
	19 Central Park West	19 Central Park East	
	9281 Avenue X	9281 Avenue X	
	22 West Farms Square	22 West Farms Square	

KEY (CORRECT ANSWERS)

1. C
2. A
3. B
4. C
5. B

———

TEST 6

Questions 1-10.

DIRECTIONS: For Questions 1 through 10, choose the letter in Column II next to the number which EXACTLY matches the number in Column I. *PRINT THE LETTER OF THE CORRECT ANSWER IN THE SPACE AT THE RIGHT.*

	COLUMN I	COLUMN II	
1.	14235	A. 13254 B. 12435 C. 13245 D. 14235	1.____
2.	70698	A. 90768 B. 60978 C. 70698 D. 70968	2.____
3.	11698	A. 11689 B. 11986 C. 11968 D. 11698	3.____
4.	50497	A. 50947 B. 50497 C. 50749 D. 54097	4.____
5.	69635	A. 60653 B. 69630 C. 69365 D. 69635	5.____
6.	1201022011	A. 1201022011 B. 1201020211 C. 1202012011 D. 1021202011	6.____
7.	3893981389	A. 3893891389 B. 3983981389 C. 3983891389 D. 3893981389	7.____
8.	4765476589	A. 4765476598 B. 4765476588 C. 4765476589 D. 4765746589	8.____

COLUMN I	COLUMN II	
9. 8679678938	A. 8679687938 B. 8679678938 C. 8697678938 D. 8678678938	9.____
10. 6834836932	A. 6834386932 B. 6834836923 C. 6843836932 D. 6834836932	10.____

Questions 11-15.

DIRECTIONS: For Questions 11 through 15, determine how many of the symbols in Column Z are exactly the same as the symbol in Column Y.
If none is exactly the same, answer A;
if only one symbol is exactly the same, answer B;
if two symbols are exactly the same, answer C;
if three symbols are exactly the same, answer D.

COLUMN Y	COLUMN Z	
11. A123B1266	A123B1366 A123B1266 A133B1366 A123B1266	11.____
12. CC28D3377	CD22D3377 CC38D3377 CC28C3377 CC28D2277	12.____
13. M21AB201X	M12AB201X M21AB201X M21AB201Y M21BA201X	13.____
14. PA383Y744	AP383Y744 PA338Y744 PA388Y744 PA383Y774	14.____
15. PB2Y8893	PB2Y8893 PB2Y8893 PB3Y8898 PB2Y8893	15.____

KEY (CORRECT ANSWERS)

1.	D	6.	A
2.	C	7.	D
3.	D	8.	C
4.	B	9.	B
5.	D	10.	D

11.	C
12.	A
13.	B
14.	A
15.	D

―――――

NAME AND NUMBER CHECKING

EXAMINATION SECTION
TEST 1

DIRECTIONS: This test is designed to measure your speed/and accuracy. You are urged to work both quickly and accurately and to do correctly as many lists as you can in the time allowed. The test consists of lists of pairs of names and numbers. Count the number of IDENTICAL pairs in each list. Then, select the correct number, 1,2, 3, 4, or 5, and indicate your choice by circling the corresponding number on your answer paper. Two sample questions are presented for your guidance, together with the correct solutions.

SAMPLE QUESTIONS   CIRCLE
CORRECT ANSWER

SAMPLE LIST A

Adelphi College - Adelphia College   1 2 3 4 5
Braxton Corp. - Braxeton Corp.
Wassaic State School - Wassaic State School
Central Islip State Hospital - Central Isllip State Hospital
Greenwich House - Greenwich House

NOTE that there are only two correct pairs - Wassaic State School and Greenwich House. Therefore, the CORRECT answer is 2.

SAMPLE LIST B

78453694	- 78453684	1 2 3 4 5
784530	- 784530	
533	- 534	
67845	- 67845	
2368745	- 2368755	

NOTE that there are only two correct pairs - 784530 and 67845. Therefore, the CORRECT answer is 2.

LIST 1

Diagnostic Clinic	- Diagnostic Clinic	1 2 3 4 5
Yorkville Health	- Yorkville Health	
Meinhard Clinic	- Meinhart Clinic	
Corlears Clinic	- Carlears Clinic	
Tremont Diagnostic	- Tremont Diagnostic	

LIST 2

73526	- 73526	1 2 3 4 5
7283627198	- 7283627198	
627	- 637	
728352617283	- 728352617282	
6281	- 6281	

LIST 3

Jefferson Clinic	- Jeffersen Clinic	
Mott Haven Center	- Mott Havan Center	
Bronx Hospital	- Bronx Hospital	
Montefiore Hospital	- Montifeore Hospital	
Beth Isreal Hospital	- Beth Israel Hospital	

LIST 4   1 2 3 4 5

936271826	- 936371826
5271	- 5291
82637192037	- 82637192037
527182	- 5271882
726354256	- 72635456

LIST 5   1 2 3 4 5

Trinity Hospital	- Trinity Hospital
Central Harlem	- Centrel Harlem
St. Luke's Hospital	- St. Lukes' Hospital
Mt.Sinai Hospital	- Mt.Sinia Hospital
N.Y.Dispensery	- N.Y.Dispensary

LIST 6   1 2 3 4 5

725361552637	- 725361555637
7526378	- 7526377
6975	- 6975
82637481028	- 82637481028
3427	- 3429

LIST 7   1 2 3 4 5

Misericordia Hospital	- Miseracordia Hospital
Lebonan Hospital	- Lebanon Hospital
Gouverneur Hospital	- Gouverner Hospital
German Polyclinic	- German Policlinic
French Hospital	- French Hospital

LIST 8   1 2 3 4 5

8277364933251	- 827364933351
63728	- 63728
367281	- 367281
62733846273	- 6273846293
62836	- 6283

LIST 9   1 2 3 4 5

King's County Hospital	- Kings County Hospital
St.Johns Long Island	- St.John's Long Island
Bellevue Hospital	- Bellvue Hospital
Beth David Hospital	- Beth David Hospital
Samaritan Hospital	- Samariton Hospital

LIST 10

		1 2 3 4 5
62836454	- 62836455	
42738267	- 42738369	
573829	- 573829	
738291627874	- 738291627874	
725	- 735	

LIST 11

		1 2 3 4 5
Bloomingdal Clinic	- Bloomingdale Clinic	
Communitty Hospital	- Community Hospital	
Metroplitan Hospital	- Metropoliton Hospital	
Lenox Hill Hospital	- Lonex Hill Hospital	
Lincoln Hospital	- Lincoln Hospital	

LIST 12

		1 2 3 4 5
6283364728	- 6283648	
627385	- 627383	
54283902	- 54283602	
63354	- 63354	
7283562781	- 7283562781	

LIST 13

		1 2 3 4 5
Sydenham Hospital	- Sydanham Hospital	
Roosevalt Hospital	- Roosevelt Hospital	
Vanderbilt Clinic	- Vanderbild Clinic	
Women's Hospltal	- Woman's Hospital	
Flushing Hospital	- Flushing Hospital	

LIST 14

		1 2 3 4 5
62738	- 62738	
727355542321	- 72735542321	
263849332	- 263849332	
262837	- 263837	
47382912	- 47382922	

LIST 15

		1 2 3 4 5
Episcopal Hospital	- Episcapal Hospital	
Flower Hospital	- Flouer Hospital	
Stuyvesent Clinic	- Stuyvesant Clinic	
Jamaica Clinic	- Jamaica Clinic	
Ridgwood Clinic	- Ridgewood Clinic	

LIST 16

		1 2 3 4 5
628367299	- 628367399	
111	- 111	
118293304829	- 1182839489	
4448	- 4448	
333693678	- 333693678	

LIST 17

Arietta Crane Farm	- Areitta Crane Farm
Bikur Chilim Home	- Bikur Chilom Home
Burke Foundation	- Burke Foundation
Blythedale Home	- Blythdale Home
Campbell Cottages	- Cambell Cottages

1 2 3 4 5

LIST 18

32123	- 32132
273893326783	- 27389326783
473829	- 473829
7382937	- 7383937
362890122332	- 36289012332

1 2 3 4 5

LIST 19

Caraline Rest	- Caroline Rest
Loreto Rest	- Loretto Rest
Edgewater Creche	- Edgwater Creche
Holiday Farm	- Holiday Farm
House of St. Giles	- House of st. Giles

1 2 3 4 5

LIST 20

557286777	- 55728677
3678902	- 3678892
1567839	- 1567839
7865434712	- 7865344712
9927382	- 9927382

1 2 3 4 5

LIST 21

Isabella Home	- Isabela Home
James A. Moore Home	- James A. More Home
The Robin's Nest	- The Roben's Nest
Pelham Home	- Pelam Home
St.Eleanora's Home	- St. Eleanora's Home

1 2 3 4 5

LIST 22

273648293048	- 273648293048
334	- 334
7362536478	- 7362536478
7362819273	- 7362819273
7362	- 7363

1 2 3 4 5

LIST 23

St.Pheobe's Mission	- St.Phebe's Mission
Seaside Home	- Seaside Home
Speedwell Society	- Speedwell Society
Valeria Home	- Valera Home
Wiltwyck	- Wildwyck

1 2 3 4 5

LIST 24

63728	- 63738	
63728192736	- 63728192738	
428	- 458	
62738291527	- 62738291529	
63728192	- 63728192	

1 2 3 4 5

LIST 25

McGaffin	- McGafin
David Ardslee	- David Ardslee
Axton Supply	- Axeton Supply Co
Alice Russell	- Alice Russell
Dobson Mfg.Co.	- Dobsen Mfg. Co.

1 2 3 4 5

KEY (CORRECT ANSWERS)

1.	3		11.	1
2.	3		12.	2
3.	1		13.	1
4.	1		14.	2
5.	1		15.	1
6.	2		16.	3
7.	1		17.	1
8.	2		18.	1
9.	1		19.	1
10.	2		20.	2

21.	1
22.	4
23.	2
24.	1
25.	2

TEST 2

DIRECTIONS: This test is designed to measure your speed and accuracy. You are urged to work both quickly and accurately and to do correctly as many lists as you can in the time allowed. The test consists of lists of pairs of names and numbers. Count the number of IDENTICAL pairs in each list. Then, select the correct number, 1, 2, 3, 4, or 5, and indicate your choice by circling the corresponding number on your answer paper. Two sample questions are presented for your guidance, together with the correct solutions.

CIRCLE
CORRECT ANSWER

LIST 1

82637381028	- 82637281028	1 2 3 4 5
928	- 928	
72937281028	- 72937281028	
7362	- 7362	
927382615	- 927382615	

LIST 2

Albee Theatre	- Albee Theatre	1 2 3 4 5
Lapland Lumber Co.	- Laplund Lumber Co.	
Adelphi College	- Adelphi College	
Jones & Son Inc.	- Jones & Sons Inc.	
S.W.Ponds Co.	- S.W. Ponds Co.	

LIST 3

85345	- 85345	1 2 3 4 5
895643278	- 895643277	
726352	- 726353	
632685	- 632685	
7263524	- 7236524	

LIST 4

Eagle Library	- Eagle Library	1 2 3 4 5
Dodge Ltd.	- Dodge Co.	
Stromberg Carlson	- Stromberg Carlsen	
Clairice Ling	- Clairice Linng	
Mason Book Co.	- Matson Book Co.	

LIST 5

66273	- 66273	1 2 3 4 5
629	- 620	
7382517283	- 7382517283	
637281	- 639281	
2738261	- 2788261	

CIRCLE
CORRECT ANSWER

LIST 6
Robert MacColl — Robert McColl   1 2 3 4 5
Buick Motor — Buck Motors
Murray Bay & Co.Ltd. — Murray Bay Co.Ltd.
L.T. Ltyle — L.T, Lyttle
A.S. Landas — A.S. Landas

LIST 7
627152637490 — 627152637490   1 2 3 4 5
73526189 — 73526189
5372 — 5392
63728142 — 63728124
4783946 — 4783046

LIST 8
Tyndall Burke — Tyndell Burke   1 2 3 4 5
W. Briehl — W, Briehl
Burritt Publishing Co. — Buritt Publishing Co.
Frederick Breyer & Co. — Frederick Breyer Co.
Bailey Buulard — Bailey Bullard

LIST 9
634 — 634   1 2 3 4 5
162837 — 163837
273892223678 — 27389223678
527182 — 527782
3628901223 — 3629002223

LIST 10
Ernest Boas — Ernest Boas   1 2 3 4 5
Rankin Barne — Rankin Barnes
Edward Appley — Edward Appely
Camel — Camel
Caiger Food Co. — Caiger Food Co.

LIST 11
6273 — 6273   1 2 3 4 5
322 — 332
15672839 — 15672839
63728192637 — 63728192639
738 — 738

LIST 12
Wells Fargo Co. — Wells Fargo Co.   1 2 3 4 5
W.D. Brett — W.D. Britt
Tassco Co. — Tassko Co.
Republic Mills — Republic Mill
R.W. Burnham — R.W. Burhnam

<table>
<tr><td></td><td></td><td>CIRCLE
CORRECT ANSWER</td></tr>
</table>

LIST 13

		1 2 3 4 5
7253529152	- 7283529152	
6283	- 6383	
52839102738	- 5283910238	
308	- 398	
82637201927	- 8263720127	

LIST 14

		1 2 3 4 5
Schumacker Co.	- Shumacker Co.	
C.H. Caiger	- C.H. Caiger	
Abraham Strauss	- Abram Straus	
B.F. Boettjer	- B.F. Boettijer	
Cut-Rate Store	- Cut-Rate Stores	

LIST 15

		1 2 3 4 5
15273826	- 15273826	
72537	- 73537	
726391027384	- 72639107384	
637389	- 627399	
725382910	- 725382910	

LIST 16

		1 2 3 4 5
Hixby Ltd.	- Hixby Lt'd.	
S. Reiner	- S. Riener	
Reynard Co.	- Reynord Co.	
Esso Gasooline Co.	- Esso Gasolene Co.	
Belle Brock	- Belle Brock	

LIST 17

		1 2 3 4 5
7245	- 7245	
819263728192	- 819263728172	
682537289	- 682537298	
789	- 789	
82936542891	- 82936542891	

LIST 18

		1 2 3 4 5
Joseph Cartwright	- Joseph Cartwrite	
Foote Food Co.	- Foot Food Co.	
Weiman & Held	- Weiman & Held	
Sanderson Shoe Co.	- Sandersen Shoe Co.	
A.M. Byrne	- A.N. Byrne	

LIST 19

		1 2 3 4 5
4738267	- 4738277	
63728	- 63729	
6283628901	- 6283628991	
918264	- 918264	
263728192037	- 2637728192073	

LIST 20

Exray Laboratories	- Exray Labratories	1 2 3 4 5
Curley Toy Co.	- Curly Toy Co.	
J. Lauer & Cross	- J. Laeur & Cross	
Mireco Brands	- Mireco Brands	
Sandor Lorand	- Sandor Larand	

LIST 21

607	- 609	1 2 3 4 5
6405	- 6403	
976	- 996	
101267	- 101267	
2065432	- 20965432	

LIST 22

John Macy & Sons	- John Macy & Son	1 2 3 4 5
Venus Pencil Co.	- Venus Pencil Co,	
Nell McGinnis	- Nell McGinnis	
McCutcheon & Co.	- McCutcheon & Co.	
Sun-Tan Oil	- Sun-Tan Oil	

LIST 23

703345700	- 703345700	1 2 3 4 5
46754	- 466754	
3367490	- 3367490	
3379	- 3778	
47384	- 47394	

LIST 24

arthritis	- athritis	1 2 3 4 5
asthma	- asthma	
endocrene	- endocrene	
gastro-enterological	- gastrol-enteralogical	
orthopedic	- orthopedic	

LIST 25

743829432	- 743828432	1 2 3 4 5
998	- 998	
732816253902	- 732816252902	
46829	- 46830	
7439120249	- 7439210249	

KEY (CORRECT ANSWERS)

1.	4	11.	3
2.	3	12.	1
3.	2	13.	1
4.	1	14.	1
5.	2	15.	2
6.	1	16.	1
7.	2	17.	3
8.	1	18.	1
9.	1	19.	1
10.	3	20.	1

21.	1
22.	4
23.	2
24.	3
25.	1

CODING
EXAMINATION SECTION
TEST 1

COMMENTARY

An ingenious question-type called coding, involving elements of alphabetizing, filing, name and number comparison, and evaluative judgment and application, has currently won wide acceptance in testing circles for measuring clerical aptitude and general ability, particularly on the senior (middle) grades (levels).

While the directions for this question-type usually vary in detail, the candidate is generally asked to consider groups of names, codes, and numbers, and, then, according to a given plan, to arrange codes in alphabetic order; to arrange these in numerical sequence; to re-arrange columns of names and numbers in correct order; to espy errors in coding; to choose the correct coding arrangement in consonance with the given directions and examples, etc.

This question-type appears to have few parameters in respect to form, substance, or degree of difficulty.

Accordingly, acquaintance with, and practice in the coding question is recommended for the serious candidate.

DIRECTIONS: Column I consists of serial numbers of dollar bills. Column II shows different ways of arranging the corresponding serial numbers.
The serial numbers of dollar bills in Column I begin and end with a capital letter and have an eight-digit number in between. The serial numbers in Column I are to be arranged according to the following rules:

First: In alphabetical order according to the first letter.

Second: When two or more serial numbers have the same first letter, in alphabetical order according to the last letter.

Third: When two or more serial numbers have the same first and last letters, in numerical order, beginning with the lowest number

The serial numbers in Column I are numbered (1) through (5) in the order in which they are listed. In Column II the numbers (1) through (5) are arranged in four different ways to show different arrangements of the corresponding serial numbers. Choose the answer in Column II in which the serial numbers are arranged according to the above rules.

Column I		Column II	
1.	E75044127B	A.	4, 1, 3, 2, 5
2.	B96399104A	B.	4, 1, 2, 3, 5
3.	B93939086A	C.	4, 3, 2, 5, 1
4.	B47064465H	D.	3, 2, 5, 4, 1

In the sample question, the four serial numbers starting with B should be put before the serial number starting with E. The serial numbers starting with B and ending with A should be put before the serial number starting with B and ending with H. The three serial numbers starting with B and ending with A should be listed in numerical order, beginning with the lowest number. The correct way to arrange the serial numbers therefore is:

3.	B93939086A	Since the order of arrangement is 3, 2, 5, 4, 1,
2.	B96399104A	the answer to the sample question is D.
5.	B99040922A	
4.	B47064465H	
1.	E75044127B	

	Column I		Column II
1.	1. D89143888P	A.	3, 5, 2, 1, 4
	2. D98143838B	B.	3, 1, 4, 5, 2
	3. D89113883B	C.	4, 2, 3, 1, 5
	4. D89148338P	D.	4, 1, 3, 5, 2
	5. D89148388B		

1.____

2.	1. W62455599E	A.	2, 4, 3, 1, 5
	2. W62455090F	B.	3, 1, 5, 2, 4
	3. W62405099E	C.	5, 3, 1, 4, 2
	4. V62455097F	D.	5, 4, 3, 1, 2
	5. V62405979E		

2.____

3.	1. N74663826M	A.	2, 4, 5, 3, 1
	2. M74633286M	B.	2, 5, 4, 1, 3
	3. N76633228N	C.	1, 2, 5, 3, 4
	4. M76483686N	D.	2, 5, 1, 4, 3
	5. M74636688M		

3.____

4.	1. P97560324B	A.	1, 5, 2, 3, 4
	2. R97663024B	B.	3, 1, 4, 5, 2
	3. P97503024E	C.	1, 5, 3, 2, 4
	4. R97563240E	D.	1, 5; 2* 3, 4
	5. P97652304B		

4.____

5.	1. H92411165G	A.	2, 5, 3, 4, 1
	2. A92141465G	B.	3, 4, 2, 5, 1
	3. H92141165C	C.	3, 2, 1, 5, 4
	4. H92444165C	D.	3, 1, 2, 5, 4
	5. A92411465G		

5.____

6.	1. X90637799S	A.	4, 3, 5, 2, 1
	2. N90037696S	B.	5, 4, 2, 1, 3
	3. Y90677369B	C.	5, 2, 4, 1, 3
	4. X09677693B	D.	5, 2, 3, 4, 1
	5. M09673699S		

6.____

7.	1. K78425174L	A.	4, 2, 1, 3, 5
	2. K78452714C	B.	2, 3, 5, 4, 1
	3. K78547214N	C.	1, 4, 2, 3, 5
	4. K78442774C	D.	4, 2, 1, 5, 3
	5. K78547724M		

7.____

8.	1. P18736652U	A.	1, 3, 4, 5, 2
	2. P18766352V	B.	1, 5, 2, 3, 4
	3. T17686532U	C.	3, 4, 5, 1, 2
	4. T17865523U	D.	5, 2, 1, 3, 4
	5. P18675332V		

8.____

9.	1. L51138101K	A.	1, 5, 3, 2, 4
	2. S51138001R	B.	1, 3, 5, 2, 4
	3. S51188111K	C.	1, 5, 2, 4, 3
	4. S51183110R	D.	2, 5, 1, 4, 3
	5. L51188100R		

9.____

Column I	Column II	
10.		10.____
1. J28475336D	A. 5, 1, 2, 3, 4	
2. T28775363D	B. 4, 3, 5, 1, 2	
3. J27843566P	C. 1, 5, 2, 4, 3	
4. T27834563P	D. 5, 1, 3, 2, 4	
5. J28435536D		
11.		11.____
1. S55126179E	A. 1, 5, 2, 3, 4	
2. R55136177Q	B. 3, 4, 1, 5, 2	
3. P55126177R	C. 3, 5, 2, 1, 4	
4. S55126178R	D. 4, 3, 1, 5, 2	
5. R55126180P		
12.		12.____
1. T64217813Q	A. 4, 1, 3, 2, 5	
2. 1642178170	B. 2, 4, 3, 1, 5	
3. T642178180	C. 4, 1, 5, 2, 3	
4. I64217811Q	D. 2, 3, 4, 1, 5	
5. T64217816Q		
13.		13.____
1. B33886897B	A. 5, 1, 3, 4, 2	
2. B38386882B	B. 1, 2, 5, 3, 4	
3. D33389862B	C. 1, 2, 5, 4, 3	
4. D33336887D	D. 2, 1, 4, 5, 3	
5. B38888697D		
14.		14.____
1. E11664554M	A. 4, 1, 2, 5, 3	
2. F11164544M	B. 2, 4, 1, 5, 3	
3. F11614455N	C. 1, 2, 1, 3, 5	
4. E11665454M	D. 1, 4, 2, 3, 5	
5. F16161545N		
15.		15.____
1. C86611355W	A. 2, 4, 1, 5, 3	
2. C68631533V	B. 1, 2, 4, 3, 5	
3. G88633331W	C. 1, 2, 5, 4, 3	
4. C68833515V	D. 1, 2, 4, 3, 5	
5. G68833511W		
16.		16.____
1. R73665312J	A. 3, 2, 1, 4, 5	
2. P73685512J	B. 2, 3, 5, 1, 4	
3. P73968511J	C. 2, 3, 1, 5, 4	
4. R73665321K	D. 3, 1, 5, 2, 4	
5. R63985211K		
17.		17.____
1. X33661222U	A. 1, 4, 5, 2, 3	
2. Y83961323V	B. 4, 5, 1, 3, 2	
3. Y88991123V	C. 4, 5, 1, 2, 3	
4. X33691233U	D. 4, 1, 5, 2, 3	
5. X38691333U		

	Column I		Column II

18.
1. B22838847W
2. B28833874V
3. B22288344X
4. B28238374V
5. B28883347V

A. 4, 5, 2, 3, 1
B. 4, 2, 5, 1, 3
C. 4, 5, 2, 1, 3
D. 4, 1, 5, 2, 3

18.____

19.
1. H44477447G
2. H47444777G
3. H74777477C
4. H44747447G
5. H77747447C

A. 1, 3, 5, 4, 2
B. 3, 1, 5, 2, 4
C. 1, 4, 2, 3, 5
D. 3, 5, 1, 4, 2

19.____

20.
1. G11143447G
2. G15133388C
3. C15134378G
4. G11534477C
5. C15533337C

A. 3, 5, 1, 4, 2
B. 1, 4, 3, 2, 5
C. 5, 3, 4, 2, 1
D. 4, 3, 1, 2, 5

20.____

21.
1. J96693369F
2. J66939339F
3. J96693693E
4. J96663933E
5. J69639363F

A. 4, 3, 2, 5, 1
B. 2, 5, 4, 1, 3
C. 2, 5, 4, 3, 1
D. 3, 4, 5, 2, 1

21.____

22.
1. L15567834Z
2. P11587638Z
3. M51567688Z
4. O55578784Z
5. N53588783Z

A. 3, 1, 5, 2, 4
B. 1, 3, 5, 4, 2
C. 1, 3, 5, 2, 4
D. 3, 1, 5, 4, 2

22.____

23.
1. C83261824G
2. C78361833C
3. G83261732G
4. C88261823C
5. G83261743C

A. 2, 4, 1, 5, 3
B. 4, 2, 1, 3, 5
C. 3, 1, 5, 2, 4
D. 2, 3, 5, 1, 4

23.____

24.
1. A11710107H
2. H17110017A
3. A11170707A
4. H17170171H
5. A11710177A

A. 2, 1, 4, 3, 5
B. 3, 1, 5, 2, 4
C. 3, 4, 1, 5, 2
D. 3, 5, 1, 2, 4

24.____

25.
1. R26794821S
2. O26794821T
3. M26794827Z
4. Q26794821R
5. S26794821P

A. 3, 2, 4, 1, 5
B. 3, 4, 2, 1, 5
C. 4, 2, 1, 3, 5
D. 5, 4, 1, 2, 3

25.____

KEY (CORRECT ANSWERS)

1.	A		11.	C
2.	D		12.	B
3.	B		13.	B
4.	C		14.	D
5.	A		15.	A
6.	C		16.	C
7.	D		17.	A
8.	B		18.	B
9.	A		19.	D
10.	D		20.	C

21.	A
22.	B
23.	A
24.	D
25.	A

TEST 2

DIRECTIONS : Questions 1 through 5 consist of a set of letters and numbers located under Column I. For each question, pick the answer (A, B, C, or D) located under Column II which contains *ONLY* letters and numbers that appear in the question in Column 1. *PRINT THE LETTER OF THE CORRECT ANSWER IN THE SPACE AT THE RIGHT.*

SAMPLE QUESTION

Column I

B-9-P-H-2-Z-N-8-4-M

Column II

A. B-4-C-3-R-9
B. 4-H-P-8-6-N
C. P-2-Z-8-M-9
D. 4-B-N-5-E-Z

Choice C is the correct answer because P,2,Z,8,M and 9 all appear in the sample question. All the other choices have at least one letter or number that is not in the question.

Column I

1. 1-7-6-J-L-T-3-S-A-2

2. C-0-Q-5-3-9-H-L-2-7

3. P-3-B-C-5-6-0-E-1-T

4. U-T-Z-2-4-S-8-6-B-3

5. 4-D-F-G-C-6-8-3-J-L

Column I

1.
A. J-3-S-A-7-L
B. T-S-A-2-6-5
C. 3-7-J-L-S-Z
D. A-7-4-J-L-1

2.
A. 5-9-T-2-7-Q
B. 3-0-6-9-L-C
C. 9-L-7-Q-C-3
D. H-Q-4-5-9-7

3.
A. B-4-6-1-3-T
B. T-B-P-3-E-0
C. 5-3-0-E-B-G
D. 0-6-P-T-9-B

4.
A. 2-4-S-V-Z-3
B. B-Z-S-8-3-6
C. 4-T-U-8-L-B
D. 8-3-T-Z-1-2

5.
A. T-D-6-8-4-J
B. C-4-3-2-J-F
C. 8-3-C-5-G-6
D. C-8-6-J-G-L

1._____

2._____

3._____

4._____

5._____

Questions 6 - 12.

DIRECTIONS: Each of the questions numbered 6 through 12 consists of a long series of letters and numbers under Column I and four short series of letters and numbers under Column II. For each question, choose the short series of letters and numbers which is entirely and exactly the same as some part of the long series.

SAMPLE QUESTION:

Column I

JG13572XY89WB14

Column II

A. 1372Y8
B. XYWB14
C. 72XY89
D. J13572

In each of choices A, B, and D, one or more of the letters and numbers in the series in Column I is omitted. Only option C reproduces a segment of the series entirely and exactly. Therefore, C is the CORRECT answer to the sample question.

6.   IE227FE383L4700

A. E27FE3
B. EF838L
C. EL4700
D. 83L470

6._____

7.   77J646G54NPB318

A. NPB318
B. J646J5
C. 4G54NP
D. C54NPB

7._____

8.   85887T358W24A93

A. 858887
B. W24A93
C. 858W24
D. 87T353

8._____

9.   E104RY796B33H14

A. 04RY79
B. E14RYR
C. 96B3H1
D. RY7996

9._____

10. W58NP12141DE07M

A. 8MP121
B. W58NP1
C. 14DEO7
D. 12141D

10._____

11. P473R365M442V5W

A. P47365
B. 73P365
C. 365M44
D. 5X42V5

11._____

12. 865CG441V21SS59

A. 1V12SS
B. V21SS5
C. 5GC441
D. 894CG4

12.____

KEY (CORRECT ANSWERS)

1. A
2. C
3. B
4. B
5. D
6. D

7. A
8. B
9. A
10. D
11. C
12. B

TEST 3

DIRECTIONS : Each question from 1 to 8 consists of a set of letters and numbers. For each question, pick as your answer from the column to the right, the choice which has *ONLY* numbers and letters that are in the question you are answering.

To help you understand what to do, the following sample question is given:

SAMPLE :   B-9-P-H-2-Z-N-8-4-M

A.   B-4-C-3-E-9
B.   4-H-P-8-6-N
C.   P-2-Z-8-M-9
D.   4-B-N-5-E-2

Choice C is the correct answer because P, 2, Z, 8, M, 9 are in the sample question. All the other choices have at least one letter or number that is not in the question.

Questions 1 through 4 are based on Column I.

Column I

1.   X-8-3-I-H-9-4-G-P-U

2.   4-1-2-X-U-B-9-H-7-3

3.   U-I-G-2-5-4-W-P-3-B

4.   3-H-7-G-4-5-I-U-8

A.   I-G-W-8-2-1

B.   U-3-G-9-P-8

C.   3-G-I-4-S-U

D.   9-X-4-7-2-H

1._____

2._____

3._____

4._____

Questions 5 through 8 are based on Column II.

Column II

5.   L-2-9-Z-R-8-Q-Y-5-7

6.   J-L-9-N-Y-8-5-Q-Z-2

7.   T-Y-3-3-J-Q-2-N-R-Z

8.   8-Z-7-T-N-L-1-E-R-3

A.   8-R-N-3-T-Z

B.   2-L-R-5-7-Q

C.   J-2-8-Z-Y-5

D.   Z-8-9-3-L-5

5._____

6._____

7._____

8._____

KEY (CORRECT ANSWERS)

1.	B	5.	B
2.	D	6.	C
3.	C	7.	A
4.	C	8.	A

TEST 4

DIRECTIONS : Questions 1 through 5 have lines of letters and numbers. Each letter should be matched with its number in accordance with the following table:

Letter	F	R	C	A	W	L	E	N	B	T
Matching Number	0	1	2	3	4	5	6	7	8	9

From the table you can determine that the letter F has the matching number 0 below it, the letter R has the matching number 1 below it, etc.

For each question, compare each line of letters and numbers carefully to see if each letter has its correct matching number. If all the letters and numbers are matched correctly in

   none of the lines of the question, mark your answer A

   only *one* of the lines of the question, mark your answer B

   only *two* of the lines of the question, mark your answer C

   all three lines of the question, mark your answer D

WBCR	4826
TLBF	9580
ATNE	3986

There is a mistake in the first line because the letter R should have its matching number 1 instead of the number 6. The second line is correct because each letter shown has the correct matching number.

There is a mistake in the third line because the letter N should have the matching number 7 instead of the number 8. Since all the letters and numbers are matched correctly in only one of the lines in the sample, the correct answer is B.

1.	EBCT	6829	1.____
	ATWR	3961	
	NLBW	7584	
2.	RNCT	1729	2.____
	LNCR	5728	
	WAEB	5368	
3.	STWB	7948	3.____
	RABL	1385	
	TAEF	9360	
4.	LWRB	5417	4.____
	RLWN	1647	
	CBWA	2843	
5.	ABTC	3792	
	WCER	5261	
	AWCN	3417	

KEY (CORRECT ANSWERS)

1. C
2. B
3. D
4. B
5. A

———

TEST 5

DIRECTIONS : Assume that each of the capital letters in the table below represents the name of an employee enrolled in the city employees retirement system. The number directly beneath the letter represents the agency for which the employee works, and the small letter directly beneath represents the code for the employees account.

Name of Employee	L	O	T	Q	A	M	R	N	C
Agency	3	4	5	9	8	7	2	1	6
Account Code	r	f	b	i	d	t	g	e	n

In each of the following Questions 1 through 10, the agency code numbers and the account code letters in Columns 2 and 3 should correspond to the capital letters in Column 1 and should be in the same consecutive order. For each question, look at each column carefully and mark your answer as follows:

If there are one or more errors in *Column 2 only,* mark your answer A,

If there are one or more errors in *Column 3 only,* mark your answer B.

If there are one or more errors in Column 2 *and* one or more errors in Column 3, mark your answer C.

If there are *NO* errors in either column, mark your answer D,

The following sample question is given to help you understand the procedure.

Column 1	Column 2	Column 3
T Q L M O C	5 8 3 7 4 6	b i r t f n

In Column 2, the second agency code number (corresponding to letter Q) should be "9", not "8". Column 3 is coded correctly to Column 1. Since there is an error only in Column 2, the correct answer is A.

	Column 1	Column 2	Column 3	
1.	Q L N R C A	9 3 1 2 6 8	i f e g n d	1._____
2.	N R M O T C	1 2 7 5 4 6	e g f t b n	2._____
3.	R C T A L M	2 6 5 8 3 7	g n d b r t	3._____
4.	T A M L O N	5 7 8 3 4 1	b d t r f e	4._____
5.	A N T O R M	8 1 5 4 2 7	d e b i g t	5._____
6.	M R A L O N	7 2 8 3 4 1	t g d r f e	6._____
7.	C T N Q R O	6 5 7 9 2 4	n d e i g f	7._____
8.	Q M R O T A	9 7 2 4 5 8	i t g f b d	8._____
9.	R Q M C O L	2 9 7 4 6 3	g i t n f r	9._____
10.	N O M R T Q	1 4 7 2 5 9	e f t g b i	10._____

KEY (CORRECT ANSWERS)

1. D
2. C
3. B
4. A
5. B

6. D
7. C
8. D
9. A
10. D

———

TEST 6

DIRECTIONS: Each of Questions 1 through 6 consists of three lines of code letters and numbers. The numbers on each line should correspond to the code letters on the same line in accordance with the table below.

Code Letter	D	Y	K	L	P	U	S	R	A	E
Corresponding Number	0	1	2	3	4	5	6	7	8	9

On some of the lines an error exists in the coding. Compare the letters and numbers in each question carefully. If you find an error or errors on

only *one* of the lines in the question, mark your answer A;
any *two* lines in the question, mark your answer B;
all *three* lines in the question, mark your answer C;
none of the lines in the question, mark your answer D.

SAMPLE QUESTION

KSRYELD   -   2671930
SAPUEKL   -   6845913
RYKADLP   -   5128034

In the above sample, the first line is correct since each code letter listed has the correct corresponding number. On the second line, an error exists because code letter K should have number 2 instead of number 1. On the third line, an error exists because the code letter R should have the number 7 instead of the number 5. Since there are errors on two of the three lines, the correct answer is B.

Now answer the following questions, using the same procedure.

1. YPUSRLD   -   1456730   1.____
    UPSAEDY   -   5648901
    PREYDKS   -   4791026

2. AERLPUS   -   8973456   2.____
    DKLYDPA   -   0231048
    UKLDREP   -   5230794

3. DAPUSLA   -   0845683   3.____
    YKLDLPS   -   1230356
    PUSKYDE   -   4562101

4. LRPUPDL   -   3745403   4.____
    SUPLEDR   -   6543907
    PKEYDLU   -   4291025

5. KEYDESR   -   2910967   5.____
    PRSALEY   -   4678391
    LSRAYSK   -   3687162

6. YESREYL   -   1967913   6.____
    PLPRAKY   -   4346821
    YLPSRDU   -   1346705

KEY (CORRECT ANSWERS)

1. A
2. D
3. C
4. A
5. B
6. A

———

POLICE SCIENCE NOTES

COLLECTION, IDENTIFICATION AND PRESERVATION OF EVIDENCE

The Definition and importance of Evidence

Definition

Evidence can be defined as "any medium of proof or probative matter, legally presented at the trial of any issue, by the participants of the trial and through the medium of witnesses, records, documents, objects, etc., for the purpose of inducing belief in the minds of the court and the jurors as to its creditability and contention." In more general terms, evidence is anything that can be legally presented to indicate the guilt of a criminal act or to aid in determining the truth about any fact in question.

Importance

The primary importance of evidence is the aid it offers in the identification of the guilty party and in his successful prosecution. Because of this, the proper collection, identification, and preservation of evidence make up a vital part of police operations. Cases may be won or lost depending upon the proficiency of the police department in this area.

Evidence is the means by which the patrolman or investigator can aid the prosecutor in giving the court a complete picture of the crime and its commission. It explains the facts that the officer uses to determine that the accused is guilty. Properly prepared and presented, evidence may serve the same purpose as taking the court and the jury to the scene of the crime and reconstructing the events which led to the commission of the crime charged.

In order to insure that this vital function is performed properly, most departments have specialists known as criminal investigators to collect, search and properly evaluate evidence. The reason for this is that such specialization saves time and leaves the patrolman free to resume his primary duties once the investigator arrives at the scene. However, since the general patrolman or the auxiliary policeman will usually be the first to arrive at the scene and therefore is crucial to the outcome of the criminal investigation, it is important that they have an adequate understanding of evidence and be skilled in its preservation and protection. The need for developing adequate investigative skills is especially crucial in those departments without a specialist and where the officers are expected to conduct their own investigation.

Classification of Evidence

Evidence may be divided into three major classifications:

DIRECT evidence directly establishes the main fact of issue. It applies immediately to the fact to be proven or disproven and is usually what a person sees, hears, or knows.

CIRCUMSTANTIAL evidence tends to prove or disprove the fact in issue by other facts leading to a presumption of the truth or falsity of the main fact. The essence here is inference-establishing a factor or circumstance from which a court may infer another fact. It may be real evidence or things which may be said to "speak for themselves." Ownership of the murder weapon, the fingerprints thereon, and the inability of the accused to account for his actions at the time of the crime would be matters of circumstantial evidence.

REAL OR PHYSICAL evidence comprises those tangible objects introduced at the trial which speak for themselves and need no explanation, just identification. Examples of real evidence would be guns, fingerprints, and bloodstains. Real evidence can be further divided into:

FIXED OR IMMOVABLE evidence which by its very nature cannot be moved from the crime scene. It includes such objects as latent fingerprints, tool marks, doors, windows, wall plaster, etc. Of course, fingerprints may be lifted, casts made of foot and tire marks, and photographs taken of the entire scene; but the actual object remains incapable of being transported to the courtroom.

MOVABLE evidence which can be preserved intact for examination at headquarters and presentation in the courtroom. This includes such objects as bullets, tools, hair, documents, clothing, and many other similar objects.

Chain of Custody - The Cardinal Rule of Evidence

In order for the evidence to be properly admitted into court, its location and holder must be accurately established from the time the officer or investigator finds the evidence until it is presented in court. If the whereabouts of the evidence cannot be established, even for a moment, the court will rule it is inadmissible. The reason for this is because if it can be shown that the evidence was out of responsible hands or unaccountable for, then it is also likely that the evidence could have been tampered with thereby negating its validity and leaving the court no alternative but to dismiss it. Therefore, in order to overcome the questions presented by the defense and to impress the judge and jury that the evidence has been properly protected, the police officer must establish an accurate "chain of custody" for each piece of evidence presented in court.

Perhaps the best method of maintaining an accurate chain of custody is through the use of receipts. If the evidence is to be out of the officer's hand for even a minute he should demand a receipt containing: the time, date, and place where the exchange occurred, to whom the evidence was given, and for what purpose. Likewise, if the officer receives any evidence for transportation or for other purposes he should fill out and give a receipt to the person giving him the evidence.

Collection of Evidence

Two points to be remembered by all personnel concerned with the collection of evidence are: (1) there, is rarely a major crime committed without some kind of evidence being left at the scene, and (2) nothing at a crime scene is too significant to be overlooked. The ultimate success of any investigation will depend on the acumen of the officers in searching the scene, recognizing evidence, and preserving it.

Preliminary Activities at the Crime Scene

The first officer at the crime scene who will usually be either the beat patrolman or the auxiliary policeman should:

1. Assist the injured when necessary.
2. Notify the proper experts and equipment to conduct a proper crime scene examination.
3. Obtain pertinent data from the witnesses and any suspects, keeping them separated if possible.
4. Use the most effective means possible to protect the crime scene from any intrusions by unauthorized personnel.
5. Arrest any perpetrators caught at or near the scene.
6. Assist the investigator when he arrives to examine the scene.

The investigator or whoever is in charge of the investigation should determine from the initial officer what has been done and what needs to be done before taking command of the situation. He will then conduct a thorough investigation of the scene and question all witnesses, victims, and suspects at the scene.

Examination of the Crime Scene

Usually the first person to be admitted to the crime scene is the photographer who will take as many photographs as necessary to insure proper coverage of the scene for further study and analysis. While the photographer is shooting the scene, the investigator will make a sketch of the scene to supplement the photographs by adding the dimensions of height, distances, and locations of the scene. Notes should also be made of the camera's position, characteristics, and the weather conditions that affect the camera's settings.

The next step in the process is the search of the crime scene area which presents various problems, especially when the area is extensive. It is essential that proper consideration be given to all aspects of the search problems before proceeding, in order that the search can be made as complete and as thorough as possible. The general organization of the search party will be determined by the size and type of the area to be covered, available personnel, and the equipment with which the party must work. It is important that the search party be divided into manageable units with each unit aware of just what area it is responsible for searching.

The number of men necessary to conduct a search will largely depends on the conditions existing at the time. Search parties may consist of as many as a hundred men, but should never be less than two. Regardless of how many people conduct the search, a careful and methodical effort must be exerted, the search should proceed according to plan, and the searchers should search for one thing at a time. If the search is going to be for fingerprints then the search should be for fingerprints only until they are all found or there is good reason to believe that there aro none. Then the search can be for bloodstains or hair, and so on down the line. The searchers may note the presence and location of one piece of evidence while looking for another piece, but the evidence noted should not be touched until the searchers are specifically looking for it. It is also a good practice to have each man responsible for a particular duty during the search. He can be a note taker, sketcher, evidence collector, or whatever else is necessary. Then when the search starts again he should be switched to another duty. This helps keep the persons alert, and insure adequate coverage of the scene. Never search a crime scene just once; always go over and over the scene until everyone is satisfied that all the evidence has been found. However, do not handle evidence more than is necessary.

The Identification of Evidence

To insure the proper chain of custody of any evidence found during the search it is necessary that every piece of evidence be marked for identification by the person who found it. Others who witness its finding should also mark the evidence of witness. If the evidence does not provide sufficient suitable area for more than a single mark it should be marked by the finding officer and witnessed by other persons. The characteristics of the mark should be recorded in the notes of the officer as well as the witnesses.

The following steps should be followed in the marking of any evidence:

1. Each bit of evidence should be appropriately marked at the time it is removed from its original position. No piece of evidence should be removed from the position in which it was found until after it has been photographed, sketched, processed for latent fingerprints, and listed in the investigator's notebook.

2. The mark "X" should never be used to identify evidence. The identifying mark should be one that is characteristic and easily identifiable. Using the written initials of the finder is considered best. The mark used and its position as well as any serial numbers or distinctive marks present on the object should be recorded in the officer's notebook for further reference.

3. Whenever possible mark the object itself, taking extreme care to prevent any destruction of the value of the evidence. Unless evidence or the article itself prohibits it, the marks made on all articles of a similar nature should be in the same direction.

4. Always mark the container in which the object is being placed as well as the object. If the object cannot be marked then seal the container and mark the seal as well as the container.

Proper marking and the keeping of notes on the evidence found during the course of an investigation will make it possible for the officer to positively identify each piece of evidence at the time it is presented in court. Using a mark which is characteristic and one that will not have been accidentally placed on the evidence, as well as knowing just where to locate the mark on the evidence is of great value to the officer witness. He will be poised and confident in his manner of handling the evidence and the judge and jury will be more impressed as to the value of the evidence presented.

Preservation and transportation of Evidence Preservation

Each article of evidence should be placed in an appropriate container depending on the nature and size of the evidence. It is recommended that the container used should be larger than necessary to normally accommodate the evidence article, so as to prevent it from being crushed or squeezed by other articles. However, the container should not be so large as to cause damage to the evidence from excessive movement. The containers should be new and clean and each article of evidence should be packed in a separate container. This is especially necessary where evidence might have foreign matter adhering to it. Should any matter adhering to the evidence fall or become separated from the article during or after packing, it will be found in the container in which the article was packed.

Transporting the Article

The transportation of the sealed evidence to the laboratory should be accompanied by the officer who collected the evidence. It has to be shipped to a laboratory, the safest and most practical method of delivery should be used and in the case of perishables, the speediest method possible should be employed.

The contents of any container should be clearly listed on the package or label. If several individual packages are packed into a single large container, the larger container should be labeled to show the content of the individual containers. This would be in addition to the labels on the individual containers. The information contained on the package should include: (1) contents of the package, (2) name of the person from whom the property was taken or where it was found, (3) the number of the case on which the evidence has a bearing, (4) the date and time it was found, (5) the name of the officer who found or received it and (6) the article to be subjected to laboratory examination, and (7) the type of examination suggested.

Storage of Evidence

One of the most important phases of maintaining the value of the evidence is its storage. The evidence must be stored in such a manner that there is no question as to actual possession.

In some departments the officer has to store the evidence in his personal locker, in others, special wall lockers are set aside for the storage of evidence with keys only available to the officer in charge of each watch and the officer who has evidence to store.

Probably the best arrangement would be for the department to have a property room with an officer from each watch in charge. After obtaining evidence the officer could then place it in the property room and receive a receipt for it. This room should have the proper facilities for storing evidence along with a strict security apparatus to keep all people except the officer of each watch in charge of it from entering.

This way the evidence could be properly stored according to its needs and the officer can be assured that the evidence has been under strict control and carefully guarded until it is needed in the laboratory or in the courtroom. He can then maintain the chain of evidence and assure the court and jury the evidence was given the best of care and handled by responsible personnel.

Conclusion

The Identification, collection, and preservation of evidence are of crucial importance to the execution of police responsibilities. The auxiliary policeman will be expected to take part in these duties when the occasion arises. His specific duties will naturally depend upon the department with which he is allied. However, in most departments because of the presence of specialists in the area of criminal investigation his main duties will be the protection of the scene and assisting the specialists where necessary. Regardless of what his duties are, the auxiliary policeman should constantly strive to gain further knowledge about this field for his own benefit. In a natural or manmade disaster he may be the only representative of the law left within an entire area and, at that time, his knowledge of proper investigative techniques will help continue law and order in society.

The auxiliary officer should remember that there are always clues at a crime scene and that everything within a crime scene is significant. Only knowledge, experience, and patience will bring these clues into the open and these take time to develop. He should never forget the importance of maintaining the chain of custody by issuing and receiving receipts. Above all, he should be constantly aware of the importance of evidence and should constantly try to improve his own skills in its identification, collection, and preservation.

———

POLICE SCIENCE NOTES

TABLE OF CONTENTS

POLICE SCIENCE NOTES

POLICE RECORDS

Records are of vital importance to a law enforcement agency, whether large or small.

A records systems should be centralized for a law enforcement agency as a whole. Separate sets of independent records in various sections or divisions of an agency or department are less useful and less desirable than centralized records. For example, a uniformed patrolman's initial report on a store burglary and a later investigative report on the same burglary prepared by the detective assigned to a case should be filed together, rather than in separate files, in the Uniform Division and the Detective Division.

1. FILING. - All reports, memoranda, letters, etc., should be filed with other documents relating to the same case or matter, in chronological order. By this means, the entire experience of the department in connection with any particular case or classification of cases or matters can be readily located for review and analysis; as desired. In addition, it simplifies locating reports when the names or subjects involved are unknown or have been forgotten.

In order to permit filing of reports, letters, memoranda and other documents in a logical, usable way (i.e., burglary cases in the burglary classification files, assaults in the assault classification files, correspondence on police uniforms with similar correspondence, in the "uniforms" classification file, etc.), it is necessary to assign classifications to reports and other documents to be filed. In order to do so, a list of "file classifications" and "file classification numbers" must be prepared and used. The classification list of each department will depend on size, specific needs, and on the variety of classifications assigned to administrative things (all police departments should have approximately the same classifications for crimes, since all are governed by the same law).

A usable classification system, for example, could begin with classifications such as: 1-Applicants, 2- Alcoholic Beverage Control Law, 3-Abandonment, 4- Accidents, etc. The system should segregate crimes into classifications by kind of crime.

Each report, memorandum, letter or document to be filed should be assigned an unvarying classification number (e.g., anthing to do with an abortion case would be marked "3"), followed by the number assigned the particular case or matter, and, if desired, a serial number.

Thus, a uniformed officer's report from an informant concerning child abandonment by a Mr. X, which would begin a new case, would be marked (on the first page only, usually at lower right) with "3" for the classification abandonment followed by a dash and a number following the number of the last case in. file (e.g. ,"3-42").

If serial numbering is desired, the report would be marked "3 - 42 - 1". The next document filed would be "3 -42 - 2," etc. The "1" shows the report is the first document put in file 3 - 42.

Files, of course, may be kept loose in individually numbered folders, or as documents permanently put together with patent fasteners of various kinds, or in files with covers, without covers, etc. A secure method should be adopted and used uniformly.

Where a classification system is used, it permits clerical filing "by the numbers," with accuracy, insuring that (for example)all abandonment cases and correspondence or other material relating to them not only go in the same place in files, but that pieces of a particular case are filed in proper order with the case and not some place else where they have to be hunted and may be lost. Procedure should be the same for any classification, whether it is "ABC Law," "Supply of Uniforms," "Vehicle Maintenance," or anything else.

2. FILING BY CLASSIFICATION AND CASE. - Reports, letters, memoranda and other documents should be identified, for filing and finding, by classification, file and serial number, in that order (e.g., 3 - 42 - 1).

a. Classification Number. - The first digit or digits of a complete "file number." It identifies the classification. In the example given, the classification number "3" indicates the case reported relates to abandonment.

b. Case Number. - The second digit or digits of the file number. It identifies the particular case concerned. Case numbers should be assigned consecutively (to initial reports or documents of cases in the same classification as they are received). Once a case has been assigned a case number, all reports in that case should carry the same number.
    In the example given, the number 42 indicates that the case is the 42nd case report in this particular classification.

    Each classification should also have a zero (0) case file and a double zero (00) case file).

    (1) Zero (0) case file. The zero case file should contain material of a non-specific nature which relates to a particular classification but does not relate to any particular case in the classification. This will be material on which no cases need be opened.

    (2) Double zero (00) file. A double zero file should be used solely for rules and instructions relating to the particular classification (not pertaining to any specific case but to the classification generally).

c. Serial Number. - A serial number indicates the order in which the report or other document was received in relation to other reports or documents in the same case-file. Serial numbers should be assigned consecutively, as the material is received for filing. They permit permanent accounting for all items in file.

Reports should be classified and assigned their classification and case numbers as they are received. Reports should, of course, be reviewed by supervisory personnel for content, errors, etc. When corrections are required, they should be brought to the attention of the responsible officer for appropriate action. If a report is satisfactory, it may then be indexed, given a serial number and filed.

Files in each classification should be kept in numerical order, behind a divider which identifies the classification.

In the file room, names of the title or heading of the first report or document filed should be indexed. Thereafter only changes or additions need be indexed. Any other names which appear in an investigation or document which are desirable to index, should be underlined by the officer or reviewing supervisor (on file copy) in red ink or pencil, with a red check mark on the first page of the report as a flag to file room personnel that there is indexing required. Supervisors should be alert to ensure that all necessary indexing is marked on file copies before they are sent to the file room. The index cards in all instances must show the name of the person or item, and the file number (classification and case numbers). Brief identifying data may also be entered (e.g., "fem, born 8/12/61").

In cases where there are any exhibits or evidence in file which are not to be retained as a permanent part of the case, a report should be placed in file showing the final disposition of them. Supervisors should ensure that evidence and exhibits are promptly disposed of when they have served their purpose. Appropriate receipts should be obtained when property is disposed of by means other than by destruction.

3. STATISTICS. - All police agencies maintain certain crime and arrest statistics covering their jurisdiction. They must submit these statistics to the Department every calendar month on forms supplied by the Department. No police agency is exempted by reason of its size or lack of personnel.

Statistics are required concerning felonies, misdemeanors and other offenses and on all persons arrested for such crimes and offenses, as specified by the Department in its statistical forms.

The statistics must show the number of offenses known to the police, how many were determined to be unfounded, and how many were "cleared by arrest." The data on arrested persons must include the county of arrest, the specific crime or offense charged, their sex, and their age. Forms and instructions may be secured directely from the Department of Corrections.

The Federal Bureau of Investigation, U. S. Department of Justice, Washington, D.C., also collects crime statistics on a monthly basis, for the national Uniform Crime Reports. Police agencies not contributing should consider doing so. Necessary details, instructions, and forms may be secured by writing to the Director, Federal Bureau of Investigation, U. S. Department of Justice, Washington, D.C., or by contacting the nearest F.B.I. office.

In order to comply with state law and to provide the basic minimum records necessary, even the smallest department must maintain a record of complaints received and a notation of action taken thereon. It must also maintain a record of persons arrested.

Such records may be maintained in their simplest form in a "blotter" or other bound volume. They are better and more useful on a separate form for each complaint and for each arrest. Separate forms may be filed in separate files by case and by classification, for various administrative uses and analyses. Such an arrangement is a bare minimum. Departments desiring to establish new and better record systems or to alter and improve old ones may obtain a "Manual of Police Records" from the Director, Federal Bureau of Investigation, U. S. Department of Justice, Washington, D.C., free of charge.

Data entered on complaint forms should always include notations as to the action taken, by whom taken, and the final disposition of the matter.

4. MOTOR VEHICLE ACCIDENTS. - The Vehicle and Traffic Law require all officers to investigate every motor vehicle accident involving a personal injury which is reported to them within five days after the accident. They must make a report of their investigation to the Commissioner of Motor Vehicles on forms furnished by the Department of Motor Vehicles.

All reports and records of any accident (not alone motor vehicle) which are kept by the State Police or by the police force of any county, city, town, or village or other district of the State, shall be open to the inspection of any person having an interest therein or his attorney or agent, except that any report or reports may be withheld from inspection if their disclosure would interfere with the investigation or prosecution of a crime involved in or connected with the accident. All departments, therefore, must keep their accident files in proper order, so that the reports may be readily located when required. This may be done by numbering and indexing or by filing by place and date of accident.

5. UNIFORM TRAFFIC TICKETS. - Under the Vehicle and Traffic Law and the Regulations of the Commissioner of Motor Vehicles, all police must use the prescribed Uniform Traffic Ticket. In addition, they are required to maintain a file of Part IV of the uniform ticket. This is one of the copies delivered to the court by the issuing officer; on it the court notes the disposition and forwards it to the department of the issuing officer.

6. JUVENILE AND YOUTH POLICE RECORDS. - All records of police relating to juvenile delinquents, persons in need of supervision or youthful offenders must be kept confidential. They may, however, be inspected upon order from the court wherein the subject was adjudged, or, without a court order, by the institution to which a youth has been committed.

Juvenile Delinquency and Persons in Need of Supervision police records must be kept by police in files separate and apart from similar files on adults. Youthful Offender files need not be separately maintained by police.

———